D0065928

GOLDEN GOODIES

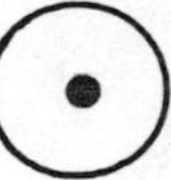

Also by Steve Propes

THOSE OLDIES BUT GOODIES
GOLDEN OLDIES

STEVE PROPES

GOLDEN GOODIES

A Guide to 50's & 60's
Popular Rock & Roll
Record Collecting

CHILTON BOOK COMPANY
Radnor, Pennsylvania

First Edition

Published in Radnor, Pa., by Chilton Book Company
and simultaneously in Don Mills, Ont., Canada
by Thomas Nelson & Sons, Ltd.

Manufactured in the United States of America

Designed by Anne Churchman

Library of Congress Cataloging in Publication Data

Propes, Steve.
Golden goodies.

1. Rock music—United States—Discography.
2. Phonorecord collecting. 3. Phonorecords—
Prices. I. Title.
ML156.4.P6P745 016.7899'12 75-6900
ISBN 0-8019-6220-X
ISBN 0-8019-6221-8 pbk.

TO

Barbara Eric

Louise Lanie

Brian Ruth

and Harry

Contents

GOLDEN GOODIES

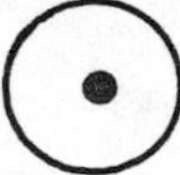

Introduction

Popular rock and roll music of the 50's and 60's was a hybrid product of several divergent sources. It was not the mainstream rhythm and blues of the 50's Clovers or Fats Domino, though it drew from their music. Nor was it the pure rockabilly of early Elvis Presley or Gene Vincent, though some popular rock and roll came from similar rockabilly origins. Compared to the rhythm and blues and rockabilly roots styles, popular rock and roll comes across as a more relaxed, innocent form of expression, which gives this music tremendous mass market appeal.

Sources

⦿

USED RECORDS

Collectors of the recorded disc, whether 45, 33 or 78 RPM or the sound of rock and roll, jazz, blues, country and western, opera, classical, folk or comedy, have long been aware that secondhand stores are excellent sources for their own specialized record wants. The condition of the records you'll find can range from freshly pressed mint to the abused and worn disc. Surprisingly, a high percentage of used records are in completely satisfactory and highly playable shape.

As with other forms of collecting, condition is a major determinant of value. Among record collectors, there are a variety of systems for condition grading. Fortunately, the following grading chart is becoming uniform for identifying the condition of 45 RPM records.

Mint (M) indicates a brand new, unplayed record —free from all defects.

Very Good (VG) is a slightly played record in excellent condition.

Good (G) is a record that has had average playing: the distortion is less prominent than the recorded performance.

Fair (F) is a record that has been played a great deal: the distortion and recorded performance are about on a par. This condition is unacceptable to most record collectors.

Poor (P) is a worn-out record. Perhaps a better description is "no damn good." The record is certainly not fit for playing, as the distortion exceeds the recorded sound.

The symbols of plus (+) and minus (-) indicate slight variation from these basic grades. Thus a record rated G+ is very similar to one in VG- condition.

Most regions and cities in the United States and Canada have a lot of used record sources such as thrift stores, auction houses, antique dealers, swap meets and garage sales. Prices at all of these locations are usually very low and can be subject to haggling. Records can cost a quarter per disc or range down to a stack of fifty singles for a dime. The price is often based on how badly the seller feels he needs to rid himself of the records.

NEW RECORDS

Retail outlets, especially the variety or drug store, have long been an excellent, basic source for discontinued, out-of-print records. Unfortunately of late, the number of these "cut-out" record sales has sharply diminished. With the advent of energy shortages, rumors of a scarcity of vinyl, the material from which records are pressed, have persisted. The strong demand for vinyl has resulted in an increase in the practice of recycling unsold records into raw vinyl for use in future pressings.

COLLECTORS, COLLECTORS' SHOPS AND COLLECTORS' JOURNALS

The prime sources for certain scarce records are stores and auctions catering specifically to record collectors. Often these stores are owned and managed by fellow record collectors who know a good deal about original labels, condition and current values. The number of these outlets, especially in the New York-Philadelphia megalopolis has mushroomed in recent years.

Several leading collectors' journals run regular auction or set sales lists. These periodicals include:

BIM BAM BOOM, Box 301, Bronx, N.Y., N.Y. 10469. This publication specializes in articles on rhythm and blues and rock and roll recordings and artists of both the 1950's and 1960's. This magazine maintains a fine, extensive auction and set sale list.

RECORD EXCHANGER, Box 2144, Anaheim, Calif. 92804. This publication is mainly concerned with rhythm and blues and rock and roll records and artists of the 1950's. Again, an extensive auction and set sale list—by consignment only. Also occasional record auction supplements and a regular listing of the best prices brought in past auctions.

ROCK MARKETPLACE, Box 253, Elmhurst-A, New York, 11380. This is the newest of the several collectors magazines, first appearing in mid-1973. The publication is designed for collectors of rock records of the 1960's and 1970's. Included are articles on the esoterica of recent domestic and imported rock. This publication has a good number of auction, set sale and want lists.

Magazines with articles geared to the record collector, but usually with no auctions, include:

SHOUT, 46 Slades Dr., Chislehurst, Kent BR 7 6JX, England. This is an excellent source for reviews and discographies on soul music of the 1960's and 1970's.

WHO PUT THE BOMP, Box 7112, Burbank, Calif., 91510. This magazine is concerned with the rock and roll of the 1950's and rock of the 1960's and 1970's.

REISSUES

Upon the withdrawal of a successful single from the current catalog, the record company may decide that the song deserves release as a "reissue." Commonly, this recording has as its flip side another hit by the same artist or by another artist from the label's roster. A listing of currently available reissues appears at the back of this book.

BOOTLEGS

An unauthorized reproduction of a recorded work is referred to as a "bootleg" or a "boot." With unprecedented interest in rare records of the 50's and 60's, this practice of recreating hard-to-get originals has sharply increased. Originally bootlegs were mainly reproductions of the most valuable and rarest recordings by such rhythm and blues groups as The Orioles, The Five Keys and The Flamingos. For many years these bootlegs sold for between $5 to $10. Recently bootleggers have turned to reproducing recordings by rock and roll, blues, rockabilly and even pop artists and the price of the discs has fallen to below $5.

Of recordings cited in this book, few have yet been bootlegged. However the aspiring collector should be wary if offered a rare mint original at a bargain price. Caution, the record may be a boot.

COLLECTORS' BOOKS

Within the past five years several books of useful interest to the rock and roll record collector have appeared on the market. Several of these books remain in print and include the following.

ROCK ENCYCLOPEDIA by Lillian Roxon, Grosset and Dunlap.

The earliest attempt at listing major and nearly major rock and roll artists from the 50's and 60's. Included are the titles of well known single recordings and album releases. Best represented are performers from the late 60's. Scant attention is paid to such 50's giants as The Platters and The Coasters or to the 60's Spector sound.

GOLDEN OLDIES: A GUIDE TO 60'S RECORD COLLECTING by Steve Propes, Chilton.

A review of the best selling and most influential rhythm and blues and rock and roll records of the 60's, from The Righteous Brothers to The Jefferson Airplane, from Roy Orbison to Bob Dylan. Features include Motown classics as well as obscurities, Phil Spector's legendary Phillies label and hard-to-get pioneer Beatles singles. Records of unusual rarity and value are noted. Over seventy 45 RPM discographies.

THOSE OLDIES BUT GOODIES: A GUIDE TO 50'S RECORD COLLECTING by Steve Propes, Macmillan.

The first "guide to record collecting" book, it contains sections on important rhythm and blues vocal groups and single artists, and sections on memorable rockabilly and rock and roll stars. There are over 50 complete discographies and numerous mini-discographies. Each section provides information on rarity and value.

THE SOUND OF THE CITY by Charlie Gillett, Outerbride and Dienstrfrey.

An exhaustively researched book with reams of valuable data on the roots of rhythm and blues and rock and roll. The book concentrates on major and obscure artists of the 50's.

BLUES RECORDS: 1943-1966 by Mike Leadbitter and Neil Slaven, Oak Publications.

There's no text, however the excellent and complete session discographies cover just about all "postwar" blues recordings.

THE DRIFTERS by Bill Millar, Collier.

The Drifters were possibly the top rhythm and blues vocal group of the 50's, in fact they were popular well into the mid-60's. By tracing the history of The Drifters, the author ties in the parallel careers and recordings of many groups, from the obscure Five Crowns to the well known Dominoes. The book is complete with a fine session discography.

ELVIS by Jerry Hopkins, Warner Paperback Library.

Though Elvis wasn't interviewed for this biographical work, the author provides an interesting career profile, early photos and an extensive 45 RPM, extended play, album and even bootleg discography.

Labels

THE MAJORS

From classical to country and western, the several major labels have been a dominant force in sales. Such a key role on the part of these majors is evident in the sales of popular rock and roll releases.

The following chart indicates the founding date of several labels, and a roster of some popular rock and roll talent with reference to the era of popularity on that label.

Label	1950-1956	1957-1962	1963-1969
Columbia, founded in the late 1880's. Subsidiary labels: Epic, Okeh.			
Talent:	The Everly Bros.	Sal Mineo (Epic) The Four Lovers (Epic)	Lou Christie The Buckinghams Jan And Dean

Label	1950-1956	1957-1962	1963-1969
		The 5 Blobs	Paul Revere And The Raiders Dion
RCA Victor, founded in 1901. Subsidiary labels: X, Vik, Groove. Talent:	Frankie Avalon (X)	The Four Lovers Neil Sedaka The Tokens Ray Peterson	Paul Anka Bobby "Boris" Pickett
Decca, founded in 1934. Subsidiary labels: Coral, Brunswick. Now known as MCA. Talent:	The Diamonds McGuire Sis. Theresa Brewer (all Coral) Bobby Helms Brenda Lee Bobby Darin Ross Bagdasarian (Coral)	Neil Sedaka	Johnny Rivers (Coral) Rick Nelson The Crests (Coral)
Capitol, founded in 1942. Talent:	The Cheers	Tommy Sands Sonny James The Royal Teens	The Beach Boys Bobby Rydell
MGM, founded in 1946. Subsidiary labels: Metro, Cub. Talent:		Mark Dinning	Lou Christie
Mercury, founded in 1947. Subsidiary labels: Wing, Smash, Phillips. Talent:	The Diamonds The Crew Cuts Georgia Gibbs	The Cheers Danny And The Juniors	The Four Seasons (Phillips)

Label	1950-1956	1957-1962	1963-1969
	The Gadabouts Ross Bagdasarian	Dickey Lee (Smash)	
ABC/Paramount, founded in 1956. Subsidiary label: Dunhill.			
Talent:	George Hamilton IV	Danny And The Juniors Paul Anka Royal Teens Billie And Lillie Tommy Roe	Del Shannon (Dunhill) Dion And The Belmonts

INDEPENDENTS

Many best selling rock and roll recordings were issued on labels established in the mid-50's and 60's. Frequently, popular rock and roll talent provided the cornerstone of success.

Independent labels often represented such regional rock and roll sounds as the surf and sunshine approach of Los Angeles and other West Coast artists, the classic "street-corner" vocal groups popular in the New York and New Jersey area or the late 50's lightweight dance beats emerging from Philadelphia.

New York Independents

Label	1950-1956	1957-1962	1963-1969
Jubilee, founded in 1948. Subsidiary label: Josie.			
Talent:		Joey Dee And The Starliters The Royal Teens	J. Frank Wilson (Josie)

Label	1950-1956	1957-1962	1963-1969
		Dion & Timberlanes	
Atlantic, founded in 1948. Subsidiary labels: Atco, Cat, East-West.			
Talent:		Bobby Darin (Atco)	Jimmy Gilmer And The Fireballs (Atco)
Cadence, founded ca. 1954.			
Talent:	The Chordettes	The Everly Bros. Johnny Tillotson	
Roulette, founded in 1956.			
Talent:		Jimmy Bowen Buddy Knox The Playmates Lou Christie	Joey Dee And The Starliters Tommy James And The Shondells
Laurie, founded in 1957.			
Talent:		Dion And The Belmonts The Mystics Dion The Belmonts	The Tokens The Buckinghams
End (The George Goldner Group), founded in 1957. Subsidiary labels: Gone, Goldisc, Cindy, Mark X. Earlier labels: Rama, Gee.			
Talent:		Dickie Goodman (Mark X) Frankie Valli & The Romans (Cindy)	The Regents (Gee)

Label	1950-1956	1957-1962	1963-1969
		Ral Donner The Four Seasons (both Gone)	
United Artists, founded ca. 1957. Subsidiary label: Unart. Talent:			Jay And The Americans The Belmonts Buddy Knox
Scepter, founded ca. 1959. Subsidiary label: Wand. Talent:		Joey Dee & The Starliters	The Kingsmen (Wand) The Crests
Warwick, founded in 1959. Talent:		The Tokens The Fireballs The Crew Cuts	
Colpix, founded in the early 60's. Talent:			John Zacherle Lou Christie
Bell, founded in the early 60's. Subsidiary labels: Amy, Mala. Talent:			Del Shannon (Amy) The Box Tops (Mala)
Buddah, founded in the mid-60's. Subsidiary labels: Super K, Kirshner, Curtom. Talent:			The Ohio Express The 1910 Fruitgum Co. The Lemon Pipers The Tokens Lou Christie

Label	1950-1956	1957-1962	1963-1969
			The Brooklyn Bridge The Archies (Kirshner) Chubby Checker

Los Angeles Independents

Imperial, founded in 1947. Subsidiary labels: Bayou, Post—now part of United Artists (see Liberty).

	1950-1956	1957-1962	1963-1969
Talent:		Ricky Nelson The Teddy Bears	Johnny Rivers The Wailers Jimmy Clanton

Dot, founded in 1951 in Tennessee—moved to Los Angeles ca. 1956.

	1950-1956	1957-1962	1963-1969
Talent:	Pat Boone Fontane Sis. Gale Storm Nervous Norvous	Tab Hunter Jan And Arnie	Jimmy Gilmer And The Fireballs

Liberty, founded in 1955. Subsidiary label: Dolphin, renamed Dolton—now part of United Artists.

	1950-1956	1957-1962	1963-1969
Talent:	David Seville	The Chipmunks Buddy Knox Bobby Vee The Fleetwoods (Dolton)	Jan And Dean Del Shannon The Bobby Fuller 4

Era, founded ca. 1956.

	1950-1956	1957-1962	1963-1969
Talent:		Larry Verne Johnny Rivers	

Warner Bros., founded ca. 1957. Subsidiary label: Reprise.

	1950-1956	1957-1962	1963-1969
Talent:		Edd "Kookie" Byrnes	Freddie Cannon Jan And Dean

Label	1950-1956	1957-1962	1963-1969
		The Nortones The Everly Bros.	Dion The Tokens Buddy Knox and Ral Donner (both Reprise)
Dore, founded ca. 1958.			
Talent:		The Teddy Bears The Zanies Jan And Dean	
Garpax, founded in the late 50's. Subsidiary label: Paxley.			
Talent:		The Hollywood Argyles (Paxley) Bobby "Boris" Pickett	
Philadelphia Independents			
Chancellor, founded in 1957.			
Talent:		Frankie Avalon Fabian Johnny Rivers	
Cameo, founded in 1957. Subsidiary label: Parkway.			
Talent:		Bobby Rydell John Zacherle The Dovells and Chubby Checker (Parkway)	The Ohio Express ? And The Mysterions The Crests Billie And Lillie
Swan, founded in 1957.			
Talent:		Freddie Cannon Dickey Doo And The Dont's Billie And Lillie	The Dovells The Royal Teens

Label	1950-1956	1957-1962	1963-1969
		Danny And The Juniors	
Jamie, founded in 1957. Subsidiary label: Guyden.			
Talent:		Johnny Rivers (Guyden)	Danny And The Juniors Neil Sedaka (both Guyden)

Several very small, short-lived independents were responsible for one or possibly two potential national hit records, but after selling or leasing the record to a major or larger independent label, these concerns soon got lost in the shuffle. Several classic rock and roll performances saw the first light of day with these "small town" companies. A few examples follow.

"A Rose And A Baby Ruth" by George Hamilton IV was first released on the Colonial label of Chapel Hill, North Carolina. It achieved hit status only after release by the ABC/Paramount label.

"Suzy Baby," a record that launched the recording career of Bobby Vee, was released originally on the Soma label of Minneapolis, yet was successful on Liberty Records.

"Hanky Panky," the first mid-60's smash hit for Tommy James And The Shondells on Roulette was originally issued by the tiny Snap label of the Minnesota area.

"At The Hop" by Danny And The Juniors was a late-50's smash hit for ABC/Paramount. The original, longer version came out on Singular of Philadelphia.

"Surfin'" by The Beach Boys was never released by a major label, even after the group's move to Capitol. This recording came out on X (not the RCA/Victor subsidiary), a true studio-in-the-garage proposition. "Surfin'" was then issued on Candix, but it never broke into a major national hit because of limited exposure and distribution. Only after joining Capitol did The Beach Boys skyrocket with smash hit success.

The Hit Record

⦿

A recording company's primary objective in releasing a popular rock and roll 45 RPM single is to score with a major hit. The common denominator found among most of the artists covered in this guide is that each achieved one or more smash hit single records.

In this section you'll find descriptions of several of the major pop rock and roll hits between the years 1955 to 1969.

1955

"Black Denim Trousers And Motorcycle Boots" by The Cheers was the first smash popular rock and roll hit which did not directly "cover" another original rhythm and blues version. The composition was a classic teenage theme—detailing a tragic motorcycle run on Highway 101 and describing the grief it caused. This recording remains a rock and roll legend.

Cover Record Hit: "I Hear You Knocking" by Gale Storm. This Smiley Lewis rhythm and blues original also proved an effective vehicle for the throaty phrasing from Miss Storm. Her cover version possessed some of the irony intended by Lewis in his recording. The honky-tonk piano helped make this a cover record which was better than average.

1956

"A Rose And A Baby Ruth" by George Hamilton IV was among the first of a series of 50's rock and roll ballads dealing with unrequited love. Hamilton's down-played approach was perfect for the melancholy lyric. This manner of sadness was indeed a popular teenage theme.

Cover Record Hit: "I Almost Lost My Mind" by Pat Boone.

1957

"Little Darlin'" by The Diamonds was probably the best of all 50's cover records. It was a far more effective recording than the original by The Gladiolas. The version by The Gladiolas was good uptempo blues, but the performance tended to lag and the recording was not crisp. In contrast, The Diamonds' arrangement was perfect, an energetic, exciting performance bringing out the best in the lyric and giving the vocal group their biggest hit. The last great cover record.

Other hits: "Love Letters In The Sand" by Pat Boone
"Diana" by Paul Anka
"At The Hop" by Danny And The Juniors

1958

"Poor Little Fool" by Ricky Nelson possessed the same mood central to George Hamilton's "A Rose And A Baby Ruth." "Poor Little Fool" was also performed in similar downcast style. This theme of unsuccessful teenage love peaked in the late 50's, largely through the recorded sentiments of Ricky Nelson and Paul Anka with his "Lonely Boy."

Other hits: "Short Shorts" by The Royal Teens

"Splish Splash" by Bobby Darin
"To Know Him Is To Love Him" by The Teddy Bears
"16 Candles" by The Crests

1959

"Venus" by Frankie Avalon provided perfect escape from an otherwise dreary popular rock and roll year. "Venus" was bright, innocent and untroubled. This 45 RPM single marked the apex for both Avalon and the Philadelphia rock and roll sound. The 60's had not quite arrived. No one was sure that rock and roll would survive.

Other hits: "Mack The Knife" by Bobby Darin
"Put Your Head On My Shoulder" by Paul Anka
"Mr. Blue" by The Fleetwoods

1960/1961

"The Twist" by Chubby Checker was an important hit record in 1960 and the source of an American life style in 1961. The recording of "The Twist" was simple, high speed rock and roll with an unusually fine dance beat. Prior to "The Twist," rock and roll dancing was mainly a bop step or a cheek-to-cheek operation. With the advent of "The Twist" and other similar steps, dancing became a form of individual expression—partners rarely touched! Rock and roll dance steps would never be the same.

Other hits (1960): "Alley Oop" by The Hollywood Argyles
"Wild One" by Bobby Rydell

Other hits (1961): "The Lion Sleeps Tonight" by The Tokens
"Runaway" by Del Shannon
"Bristol Stomp" by The Dovells

1962

"Monster Mash" by Bobby "Boris" Pickett was

mainstream novelty. The recording possessed a rocking dance step with original lyrics meant as a bit of a put-down of the plethora of dance records glutting the early 60's record charts.

Other hits: "Palisades Park" by Freddie Cannon
"Breaking Up Is Hard To Do" by Neil Sedaka

1963

"Surf City" by Jan And Dean epitomized this era of surf rock. Though not the best rock and roll release of this surfin' and sun genre, it was an appealing and extremely popular record for Jan And Dean.

Other hits: "Sugar Shack" by Jimmy Gilmer And The Fireballs
"Louie Louie" by The Kingsmen

1964

"Memphis" was Johnny Rivers' remake of the Chuck Berry rocker (Chess 1729) and introduced the live, discotheque sound to popular rock and roll recordings. This "go-go" beat replaced the waning twist as the focal point for live dancing.

Other hits: "Last Kiss" by J. Frank Wilson
"Come A Little Bit Closer" by Jay And The Americans

1965

"Lightning Strikes" by Lou Christie was exciting, pulsating rock and roll with a not-so-obscure, willing sexual message. During the still prudish mid-60's, this record brought a brief wave of suppression down upon alleged double entendre rock and roll.

Other hits: "Kicks" by Paul Revere And The Raiders
"California Girls" by The Beach Boys

1966

"I'm A Believer" by The Monkees was an early

major bubble gum music hit. The recording also happened to be easygoing, first-class rock and roll.

Other hit: "Hanky Panky" by The Shondells, later known as Tommy James And The Shondells

1967

"The Letter" by The Box Tops was again fine rock and roll, this time with a harder edge. Popular rock and roll was in no sense "heavy," yet this 45 RPM single possessed some of the feel of hard rock.

Other hit: "Hey Baby (They're Playing Our Song)" by The Buckinghams

1968

"Abraham, Martin And John" revealed a softer, folk side of Dion. This original ballad, composed during the tumultuous late 60's, grieved over the loss of kind and good Americans.

Other hit: "Bottle Of Wine" by The Fireballs

1969

"Sugar Sugar" by The Archies was excellent preteen bubble gum rock and roll. This very young audience had arrived as a major and growing market for rock and roll.

Other hit: "Crystal Blue Persuasion" by Tommy James And The Shondells

Themes in Popular Rock and Roll

MISUNDERSTOOD AND UNREQUITED LOVE

George Hamilton IV's "A Rose And A Baby Ruth" described his offerings of apology after breaking up with his girl—the song was a grabber, rendered with feeling.

Some of Paul Anka's best and most overwhelming compositions had to do with this downbeat subject. Anka's "Diana" was about his love for an older woman. This was an affair that just couldn't work out. "Lonely Boy" was a desperate prayer for help in overcoming his need for love. Paul Anka rendered these self-composed songs with a deep, deep anxiety that could be clearly felt in his voice.

Ricky Nelson didn't appear anxious at all in his "Stood Up." You had the firm impression that he could muddle through this situation. In Nelson's "Poor Little Fool," he had broken the hearts of several girlfriends, but this time it was he who was fooled. Ricky Nelson didn't communicate deep depression—there was no latent suicide or question of survival.

Dion And The Belmonts preferred to keep loneliness a well-hidden secret in "No One Knows" and "Don't Pity Me." A similar desire for private depression was expressed in The Fleetwoods' "Mr. Blue." In both "Mr. Blue" and "No One Knows," the ex-girlfriend is out having an absolutely great time while the boyfriend is left to sulk and suffer.

Bobby Vee is hardly despondent over the loss of his love in "Take Good Care Of My Baby." You didn't worry, he could take it. Del Shannon was left alone in "Runaway," but he soon got even when his girl was spurned in "Hats Off To Larry."

TEENAGE LOVE AND PAIN

The theme of teenage pain bore close ties to the theme of spurned love, however this suffering was caused more by the parental generation's rejection and misunderstanding.

Again, George Hamilton IV knew that even a teenager could really fall in love. Unfortunately his parents didn't agree in "Why Don't They Understand." Tommy Sands asserted that his feelings of love were by far more profound than a mere "Teenage Crush." Paul Anka similarly rejected the term "Puppy Love" as not truly describing his own feelings. Ricky Nelson knew his thoughts were somehow different in "Young Emotions."

Pat Boone's approach was detached and benevolent towards the generation of teenagers in his "Twixt Twelve And Twenty."

Dion And The Belmonts finally found love in "A Teenager In Love," but the pain made them question why they had to suffer through the experience. Dion as a single artist found himself again in solitude and away from home in "Lonely Teenager."

Happily, though, Paul Anka in 'Teen Commandments" closed the generation gap by devising a set of rules for understanding the mysterious older generation.

DEFIANCE AND REBELLION

The theme of restless rebellion was a favored popular rock and roll topic throughout the 50's and 60's.

"Black Denim Trousers And Motorcycle Boots" was The Cheers' second person narrative of the adventures and an inevitably tragic fate befalling a restless motorcycle rider. The moral depicted in this early 50's piece was clear: the privilege to rebel always exacts a price.

Dion identified himself as a footloose and unfettered spirit in "The Wanderer," similar to Ricky Nelson's self-portrayal in "Travelin' Man." Fabian created a mood of free-swinging manliness in "I'm A Man," "Tiger," "Turn Me Loose" and "Hound Dog Man."

The Beach Boys translated the theme of restlessness into a situation of conflict between generations in "Fun Fun Fun." The resolution of this tale was characteristically happy.

"Kicks" by Paul Revere And The Raiders described the anarchy of hard drug use. The harsh rock tone of this piece demanded that rebellion through drugs be abandoned.

In the iconoclastic spirit of The Kinks' "A Well Respected Man," The Monkees took a harmless poke at a mundane middle class weekend in their "Pleasant Valley Sunday."

DEATH AND DEPRESSION

The Nervous Norvous release of "Transfusion"

looked at highway tragedy and implied death in a deadpan joking style which, in the innocent 50's, was totally unique to rock and roll music. Though "Transfusion" was essentially a comedy release, it plainly confronted the subject of bloody violence. This style recording was not to return in such a successful form.

However, by the late 50's, a whole procession of rock and roll 45 RPM singles appeared, each with a heart-tugging, melancholy ending by death. They were created for a seemingly insatiable audience.

The central character in "Black Denim Trousers And Motorcycle Boots" died at record's end, but there was no message of overwhelming sadness.

In contrast, late 50's death rock releases were designed to milk the last drop of compassion for a relationship of love, unfairly crushed through death of one partner. Only the method of extinction differed. Several of these recordings included death through a car versus train wreck, including Mark Dinning's "Teen Angel" (MGM 12846) and J. Frank Wilson's "Last Kiss" (Josie 923); through suicide in Dickey Lee's "Patches" (Smash 1758); through a stock car racing mishap in Ray Peterson's "Tell Laura I Love Her" (RCA 7745); and through airliner crash in The Everly Brothers' "Ebony Eyes"—all major hit singles.

Of similar effect was Tommy Dee's tribute to the passing of Buddy Holly, Richie Valens and The Big Bopper in "Three Stars" (Crest 1057).

"HEY, VENUS"

In the era of the 50's, the accepted view of teenage girls was that they should be demure, yet sociable, certainly not "easy" or "loose." They should be attractive to the opposite sex—at arm's length.

Buddy Knox's "Party Doll" and Ricky Nelson's "Be Bop Baby" portrayed such idealized sought-after high school girls. After all, this girl could attract Ricky, thus the ideal teenage coed image was affirmed.

Bobby Darin created his "Queen Of The Hop" and a later "Dream Lover" to wish for. A further accounting of distinctive girl-themed singles includes Neil Sedaka's "Oh, Carol" and "Calendar Girl," Tommy Roe's "Sheila," Bobby Vee's "Suzy Baby," among a whole company of others.

Perhaps, though, the essential theme was best personified through Frankie Avalon's delicate "Venus"—an image of the faultless female.

In opposition, whenever a female popular rock and roll singer sang of her boyfriend, he was more often than not an oddball character, such as Annette's "Tall Paul" or the strange boyfriend described in Dodie Steven's "Pink Shoe Laces" (Crystalette 724).

SCHOOL

The listening and buying audience for popular rock and roll of the 50's and 60's was made up of high school, junior high, elementary and even nursery school inmates.

High school was the setting for several of the most successful rock and roll records of both decades. In 1957, Ricky Nelson found himself patiently "Waitin' In School" for his day of fun at the malt shop to begin.

Bobby Rydell was able to make the best of his high school day by fancifully dreaming of luxurious improvements in his "Swingin' School."

Freddie Cannon's "Abigail Beecher (Our History Teacher)" was a far-out faculty bopper in fine rock and roll style.

Several years later, The Beach Boys strongly advocated school spirit in cheerleading style in "Be True To Your School."

HANGOUTS

After school and late night hangouts were also found in the lyrics of popular rock and roll records.

Most of these popular locales were of the fictional variety, such as Jimmy Gilmer And The Fireballs' "Sugar Shack." Jan And Dean were considerably more ambitious—they created entire teenage communities in pursuit of specialized diversion through "Surf City" and the follow-up "Drag City."

Freddie Cannon sang about a real life fun zone in the rocking "Palisades Park." In contrast, Annette never sang about the much better known Disneyland, though she recorded exclusively for the Disney house label.

DRESS STYLES

Style-conscious teenagers of the very late 50's were able to identify several current fashion trends through lyrics of rock and roll records.

The pace was set by the classic release, "Short Shorts," by the Royal Teens, along with the similar follow-up recording of "Leotards." The Royal Teens touched upon a more unusual fashion, the use of a "Big Name Button."

Gerry Granahan rejected out-of-hand a new 1958 fashion look in his "No Chemise Please" (Sunbeam 102).

The practice of advertising a boyfriend's identity was the theme of Annette's "First Name Initial."

NOVELTY LYRICS

Novelty recordings covered widely diverse subjects with a variety of approaches—from the innocent voices of animal characters to calculated ghoulish narratives.

The monster creation was a resoundingly effective subject area. Most successful in this form were John Zacherle's outrageously sly "Dinner With Drac," positively not for the weak of stomach, and Bobby "Boris" Pickett's danceable "Monster Mash." A minor 1958 hit for The Zanies was "The Blob" (Dore 785), also performed by The Five Blobs (Columbia 41250), an early Burt Bacharach composition taken from a sci-fi movie with the same title. "Batman, Wolfman, Frankenstein And Dracula" by The Diamonds was designed to sum up the use of these rocking monsters.

Cartoon and comic-strip characters often seemed made to order for rock and roll interpretations. Probably the best of comic-strip recordings was the Hollywood Argyles' "Alley Oop," a major hit. The Kingsmen neatly adapted their bedlam rock and roll to the simplistic lyrics of "Anny Fanny" and "Jolly Green Giant." Jan And Dean's "Batman" is an evergreen comic-strip hero translated into a most popular late 60's TV series from which the recording was drawn.

By the late 60's, the process was reversed as rock and roll artists were themselves changed into cartoon form by virtue of television's "The Archies." Also adapted into cartoon characters by this process were the quite popular Jackson 5 and The Osmonds.

The Cover Record

The practice of "covering" a hit record can be traced to recordings of the late 30's and early 40's, when several artists would record similar arrangements of a currently popular composition. Covers were not just popular renditions of rhythm and blues material, they could be popular versions of country and western hits, or even a rhythm and blues cover of a best selling rhythm and blues hit. An early example of a rhythm and blues cover is "The Honeydripper" (Exclusive 207), by Joe Liggins, released in 1945 and soon covered by Jimmie Lunceford And The Delta Rhythm Boys (Decca 23451), Roosevelt Sykes (Blue-Bird 0737) and Sammy Franklin And The Atomics (Black And White 101), among others.

In the early and mid-50's, rhythm and blues compositions generally received first national exposure only after being translated into the earliest embodiment of rock and roll: the cover record. This cover record transformed relatively primitive rhythm and blues material into more subdued and relaxed pop arrangements.

The pop rock and roll cover thrived for the four years between 1954 through 1957. During this period, the sounds of rhythm and blues and harder rockabilly and rock and roll were not fully accepted on their own artistic merits, thus the music required "cleaning" or "legitimatizing" by the covering artist.

Examples of rhythm and blues originals follow, together with the consistently better selling popular cover versions—better selling, at least, during the heydey of the cover era. Among these cover records can be found several of the biggest hits of the early and mid-50's. Among the rhythm and blues versions can be found some of the more sought-after records by contemporary record collectors.

1954

Title	*Original Version*	*Cover Version*
"Bazoom (I Need Your Loving)"	The Charms DeLuxe 6076	The Cheers Capitol 2921
"Sh Boom"	The Chords Cat 104	The Crew Cuts Mercury 70404
"Oop Shoop"	Shirley Gunter And The Queens Flair 1040	The Crew Cuts Mercury 70443
"Hearts Of Stone"	The Jewels R&B 1301	The Fontane Sisters Dot 15265
"Rock Love"	Lula Reed King 4767	The Fontane Sisters Dot 15333
"You're Mine"	Shirley Gunter And The Queens Flair 1060	The Fontane Sisters Dot 15333
"Most Of All"	The Moonglows Chess 1589	The Fontane Sisters Dot 15352

Title	*Original Version*	*Cover Version*
"Rolling Stone"	The Marigolds Excello 2057	The Fontane Sisters Dot 15370
"Mambo Baby"	Ruth Brown Atlantic 1044	Georgia Gibbs Mercury 70473
"Goodnight Sweetheart, Goodnight"	The Spaniels Veejay 107	The McGuire Sisters Coral 61187
1955		
"Two Hearts"	The Charms DeLuxe 6065	Pat Boone Dot 15338 The Crew Cuts Mercury 70598
"Ain't It A Shame"	Fats Domino Imperial 5348	Pat Boone Dot 15377
"At My Front Door"	The El Dorados Vee Jay 147	Pat Boone Dot 15422
"Gee Whittakers"	The Five Keys Capitol 3267	Pat Boone Dot 15422
"Pledging My Love"	Johnny Ace Duke 136	Theresa Brewer Coral 61362
"Whadaya Want"	The Robins Spark 110	The Cheers Capitol 3019
"I Must Be Dreamin'"	The Robins Spark 116	The Cheers Capitol 3146
"Earth Angel"	The Penguins Dootone 348	The Crew Cuts Mercury 70527
"Ko Ko Mo"	Gene And Eunice Combo 64	The Crew Cuts Mercury 70527
"Chop Chop Boom"	The Danderliers States 147 Jack McVea & Savoys Combo 90	The Crew Cuts Mercury 70597

Title	*Original Version*	*Cover Version*
"Don't Be Angry"	Nappy Brown Savoy 1155	The Crew Cuts Mercury 70597
"A Story Untold"	The Nutmegs Herald 452	The Crew Cuts Mercury 70634
"Gum Drop"	The Charms DeLuxe 6090	The Crew Cuts Mercury 70668
"Angels In The Sky"	The Monarchs Wing 90040	The Crew Cuts Mercury 70741
"Nip Sip"	The Clovers Atlantic 1073	The Diamonds Coral 61502
"Adorable"	The Colts Vita 112 The Drifters Atlantic 1078	The Fontane Sisters Dot 15428
"Daddy-O"	Bonnie Lou King 4835	The Fontane Sisters Dot 15428
"Seventeen"	Boyd Bennett & Rockets King 1470	The Fontane Sisters Dot 15383
"Two Things I Love"	The Cardinals Atlantic 1067	The Gadabouts Wing 90008
"Oochie Pachi"	The Platters King 4773	The Gadabouts Mercury 70581
"Tweedle Dee"	LaVern Baker Atlantic 1047	Georgia Gibbs Mercury 70517
"Dance With Me Henry" (orig. title "The Wall-flower")	Etta James & Peaches Modern 947	Georgia Gibbs Mercury 70572
"Sincerely"	The Moon-glows Chess 1581	The McGuire Sisters Coral 61323
"I Hear You Knocking"	Smiley Lewis Imperial 5356	Gale Storm Dot 15412
"Teenage Prayer"	Dolly Cooper Modern 977	Gale Storm Dot 15436

Title	*Original Version*	*Cover Version*
1956		
"Tutti Frutti"	Little Richard Specialty 561	Pat Boone Dot 15443
"I'll Be Home"	The Flamingos Checker 830	Pat Boone Dot 15443
"Long Tall Sally"	Little Richard Specialty 572	Pat Boone Dot 15457
"I Almost Lost My Mind"	Ivory Joe Hunter MGM 10578	Pat Boone Dot 15472
"Chains Of Love"	Joe Turner Atlantic 939	Pat Boone Dot 15490
"A Tear Fell"	Ivory Joe Hunter Atlantic 1086	Theresa Brewer Coral 61590
"Bo Weevil"	Fats Domino Imperial 5375	Theresa Brewer Coral 61590
"Seven Days"	Clyde McPhatter Atlantic 1081	The Crew Cuts Mercury 70782
"That's Your Mistake"	The Charms DeLuxe 6091	The Crew Cuts Mercury 70782
"Out Of The Picture"	The Robins Whippet 200	The Crew Cuts Mercury 70840
"Why Do Fools Fall In Love"	The Teenagers Gee 1012	The Diamonds Mercury 70790 Gale Storm Dot 15448
"You Baby You"	The Cleftones Gee 1000	The Diamonds Mercury 70790
"Church Bells May Ring"	The Willows Melba 102	The Diamonds Mercury 70835
"Little Girl Of Mine"	The Cleftones Gee 1011	The Diamonds Mercury 70835
"Love Love Love"	The Clovers Atlantic 1094	The Diamonds Mercury 70889
"Every Night About This Time"	The Ink Spots Decca 29957	The Diamonds Mercury 70889
"Ka Ding Dong"	The G-Clefs Pilgrim 715	The Diamonds Mercury 70934

Title	*Original Version*	*Cover Version*
"A Thousand Miles Away"	The Heartbeats Hull 720	The Diamonds Mercury 71021
"Eddie My Love"	The Teen Queens RPM 453	The Fontane Sisters Dot 15450 The Chordettes Cadence 1284
"I'm In Love Again"	Fats Domino Imperial 5386	The Fontane Sisters Dot 15462
"Please Don't Leave Me"	Fats Domino Imperial 5240	The Fontane Sisters Dot 15501
"Still"	LaVern Baker Atlantic 1104	The Fontane Sisters Dot 15501
"Stranded In The Jungle"	The Jayhawks Flash 109 The Cadets Modern 994	The Gadabouts Mercury 70898
"Too Much Monkey Business"	Chuck Berry Chess 1635	The Gadabouts Mercury 70978
"Goodnight My Love"	Jesse Belvin Modern 1005	The McGuire Sisters Coral 61748
"Ivory Tower"	The Charms DeLuxe 6093	Gale Storm Dot 15458
"Lucky Lips"	Ruth Brown Atlantic 1125	Gale Storm Dot 15539
1957		
"Empty Arms"	Ivory Joe Hunter Atlantic 1128	Theresa Brewer Coral 61805
"You Send Me"	Sam Cooke Keen 4013	Theresa Brewer Coral 61898
"Young Love"	Sonny James Capitol 3602	The Crew Cuts Mercury 71022

Title	*Original Version*	*Cover Version*
		Tab Hunter Dot 15533
"Susie Q"	Dale Hawkins Checker 863	The Crew Cuts Mercury 71125
"Little Darlin'"	The Gladiolas Excello 2101	The Diamonds Mercury 71060
"Silhouettes"	The Rays Cameo 117	The Diamonds Mercury 71197
"Daddy Cool"	The Rays Cameo 117	The Diamonds Mercury 71197
"Words Of Love"	Buddy Holly Coral 61852	The Diamonds Mercury 71128
"I'm Walkin'"	Fats Domino Imperial 5428	Ricky Nelson Verve 10047

As the preceding chart makes clear, the cover record was enormously beneficial to the recording careers of Pat Boone on the Dot label, The Crew Cuts, The Diamonds and The Gadabouts on Mercury and the Cheers on Capitol.

PAT BOONE

Pat Boone began his recording career as a country and western vocalist with the small Republic label. However, Pat Boone's historic success came with a long string of both cover and original composition hit releases on the Dot label. Boone was among the earliest—and was possibly the most successful—of the 50's cover artists. He was able to turn relatively primitive rhythm and blues recordings into sweetly subdued national pop hits.

Pat Boone's ability to dilute the intensity of an original rhythm and blues performance is most strikingly apparent in his smoothed out renditions of two Little Richard stompers, "Tutti Frutti" and "Long Tall Sally."

By 1957, the instant hit appeal of the cover record was largely diminished. This was quickly apparent in Theresa Brewer's dismal flop, "You Send Me"—a smash hit for Sam Cooke. At this juncture, Pat Boone met even greater success with two original compositions, the sweetly romantic ballads "Love Letters In The Sand" and "April Love"—his very biggest hits. The year 1957 represented the apex of popularity for Boone, complete with his own television variety show on the ABC network.

Pat Boone continued well into the early 60's with occasional hits, such as 1958's "Sugar Moon" and "If Dreams Came True"; "Twixt Twelve And Twenty" in 1959; the ominous "Moody River" in 1961 and the novelty "Speedy Gonzales" in 1962.

Into the very late 60's, Pat Boone had opted for the folk rock approach so successful for such fellow 50's pop rock and roll stars as Ricky Nelson and Bobby Darin.

Values

Pat Boone's releases on the Republic label are fairly scarce on 45 RPM and can bring around $5 to $10 from a confirmed Boone collector. Most of the early Dot label efforts (up to Dot 15490) are valued about $2 apiece.

Discography

Republic

7062	"Remember To Be Mine"	
7084	"I Need Someone"/"Loving You Madly"	ca. 1952
7119	"I Need Someone"/"My Heart Belongs To You"	

Dot

15338	"Two Hearts"/"Tra La La"	1954
15377	"Ain't That A Shame"/"Tennessee Saturday Night"	1955
15422	"At My Front Door"/"No Other Arms"	
15435	"Gee Whittakers"/"Take The Time"	
15443	"Tutti Frutti"/"I'll Be Home"	1956
15457	"Long Tall Sally"/"Just As Long As I'm With You"	
15472	"I Almost Lost My Mind"/"I'm In Love With You"	
15490	"Chains Of Love"/"Friendly Persuasion"	
15521	"Don't Forbid Me"/"Anastasia"	
15545	"Why Baby Why"/"I'm Waiting Just For You"	1957
15570	"Love Letters In The Sand"/"Bernadine"	
15602	"Remember You're Mine"/"There's A Gold Mine In The Sky"	
15660	"April Love"/"When The Swallows Come Back To Capistrano"	
15690	"It's Too Soon To Know"/"A Wonderful Time Up There"	1958
15750	"Sugar Moon"/"Cherie I Love You"	
15785	"If Dreams Came True"/"That's How Much I Love You"	
15825	"For My Good Fortune"/"Gee But Its Lonely"	
15840	"I'll Remember Tonight"/"The Mardi Gras March"	
15888	"With The Wind And The Rain In Your Hair"/"Good Rockin' Tonight"	1959
15914	"The Wang Dang Taffy Apple Tango"/"For A Penny"	
15955	"Twixt Twelve And Twenty"/"Rock Boll Weevil"	
15982	"Fools Hall Of Fame"/"Brightest Wishing Star"	
16006	"Beyond The Sunset"/"My Faithful Heart"	
16048	"New Lovers"/"Words"	1960

16073 "Walking The Floor Over You"/"Spring Rain"
16122 "Delia Gone"/"Candy Sweet"
16152 "Dear John"/"Alabam"
16176 "There's A Moon Out Tonight"/"The Exodus Song" 1961
16209 "Moody River"/"A Thousand Years"
16244 "Big Cold Wind"/"That's My Desire"
16284 "Johnny Will"/"Just Let Me Dream"
16312 "I'll See You In My Dreams"/"Pictures In The Fire" 1962
16349 "Quando Quando Quando"/"Willing And Eager"
16368 "Speedy Gonzales"/"The Locket
16391 "Ten Lonely Guys"/"Lover's Lane"
16416 "Mexican Joe"/"In The Room"
16439 "Meditations"/"Days Of Wine And Roses" 1963
16474 "Always You And Me"/"Main Attraction"
16494 "Tie Me Kangaroo Down Sport"/ "I Feel Like Crying"
16516 "Never Put It In Writing"/"I Like What You Do"
16525 "Mister Moon"/"Love Me"
16559 "Some Enchanted Evening"/"That's Me"
16576 "Never Put It In Writing"/"I Like What You Do"
16598 "I Understand"/"Rosemarie" 1964
16626 "Side By Side"/"I'll Never Be Free" (by Pat & Shirley Boone)
16641 "Sincerely"/"Don't You Just Know It"
16658 "Little Honda"/"Beach Girl"
16668 "Goodbye Charlie"/"Love, Who Needs It"
16699 "Blueberry Hill"/"Heartaches"
16707 "Baby Elephant Walk"/"Say Goodbye"
16728 "Crazy Arms"/"Pearly Shells"
16738 "Mickey Mouse"/"Time Marches On"
16754 "With My Eyes Wide Open I'm Dreaming"/"Rainy Days"
16785 "Meet Me Tonight In Dreamland"

16808	"A Man Alone"/"Run To Me Baby"	1965
16825	"As Tears Go By"/"Judith Home"	
16836	"It Seems Like Yesterday"/"Well Remembered, Highly Thought Of Love Affair"	
16871	"Don't Put Your Feet In The Lemonade"/ "Five Miles From Home"	
16933	"Wish You Were Here Buddy"/"Love For Love"	1966

THE CREW CUTS

The Crew Cuts had very early recorded success with pop-styled interpretations based on the just emerging rhythm and blues form with the songs "Sh Boom" and "Earth Angel." These two cover records, both pioneer rhythm and blues hits, were pop hits. Each was a romantic ballad, well suited to the unabashed middle-of-the-road pop style of The Crew Cuts. By 1956, this non-rock and roll approach of The Crew Cuts had faded in popularity. The Diamonds and other groups, who were capable of stronger rock and roll performances, created the dominant style of the late and mid-50's.

Values

On the original Mercury label, 45 RPM releases by The Crew Cuts are rarely worth more than $2 or $3.

Discography

Mercury

70341	"Crazy About Ya Baby"/"Angela Mia"	1954
70404	"Sh Boom"/"I Spoke Too Soon"	
70443	"Oop Shoop"/"Do Me Good Baby"	

70490 "All I Wanna Do"/"The Barking Dog"
70491 "Dance Mr. Snowman Dance"/"Twinkle Toes"
70494 "The Whiffenpoof Song"/"Varsity Drag" 1955
70527 "Earth Angel"/"Ko Ko Mo"
70597 "Chop Chop Boom"/"Don't Be Angry"
70598 "Two Hearts, Two Kisses"/"Unchained Melody"
70634 "A Story Untold"/"Carmen's Boogie"
70668 "Gum Drop"/"Song Of The Fool"
70668 "Gum Drop"/"Present Arms"
70710 "Slam Bam"/"Are You Having Any Fun"
70741 "Angels In The Sky"/"Mostly Martha"
70782 "Seven Days"/"That's Your Mistake" 1956
70840 "Out Of The Picture"/"Honey Hair, Sugar Lips, Eyes Of Blue"
70890 "Tell Me Why"/"Rebel In Town"
70922 "Bei Mir Bist Du Schon"/"Thirteen Going On Fourteen"
70977 "Love In A Home"/"Keeper Of The Flame"
70988 "Halls Of Ivy"/"Varsity Drag"
71022 "Young Love"/"Little By Little" 1957
71076 "Whatever, Whenever, Whoever"/"Angelus"
71125 "Susie-Q"/"Such A Shame"
71168 "I Sit In My Window"/"Hey, You Face"
71223 "Be My Only Love"/"I Like It Like That"

Warwick
558 "Over The Mountain"/"Searchin'" 1959
623 "Legend Of Gunga Din"/"Number One With Me"

THE CHEERS

One of the very first popular rock and roll groups, The Cheers were a trio consisting of one female and two male vocalists. They were at first quite successful with two cover records, "Bazoom (I Need Your Lovin')" and "Whadaya Want." However, by far the best remembered work by The Cheers was the dramatic, high-speed "Black Denim Trousers And Motorcycle Boots," an early motorcycle epic with a predictably tragic ending. This recording is also notable as the first national hit for the well-known Leiber And Stoller writing team, already responsible for many earlier rhythm and blues classics, including "Bazoom" and "Whadaya Want." The Cheers had an unexpectedly short lifespan despite their impressive hit output. They did manage to turn "Black Denim Trousers And Motorcycle Boots" into an early rock and roll classic.

Values

Recordings by The Cheers on Capitol generally bring $3 to $5 on 45 RPM.

Discography

Capitol		
2921	"Bazoom (I Need Your Lovin')"/ "Arivederci"	1954
3019	"Whadaya Want"/"Bernie's Tune"	1955
3075	"Blueberries"/"Can't We Be More Than Friends"	
3146	"I Must Be Dreamin'"/"Fancy Meeting You Here"	
3219	"Black Denim Trousers And Motorcycle Boots"/"Some Night In Alaska"	
3353	"Chicken"/"Do Do Anything"	1956
Mercury		
71083	"Big Feet"/"Chug Chug Toot Toot"	1957
71100	"Two Hearts"	

THE GADABOUTS

Mercury Records experienced impressive success with the mid-50's cover record by virtue of a long hit string from both The Diamonds and The Crew Cuts. The Gadabouts were the third Mercury label cover group, with such single releases as "Oochi Pachi," "Stranded In The Jungle" and "Too Much Monkey Business." However, the most effective release by the latter group was an excellent ballad "All My Love Belongs To You." Despite several professional releases, The Gadabouts never had a topnotch hit.

Values

Singles by The Gadabouts are generally valued about $3 each.

Discography

Mercury

70495	"By The Waters Of The Minnie Tonka"/ "Guiseppe Mandolino"	1954
70581	"Oochi Pachi"/"You Make My Heart Go Boom Boom"	1955
70823	"All My Love Belongs To You"/"Busy Body Rock"	1956
70898	"Stranded In The Jungle"/"Blues Train"	
70978	"Too Much Monkey Business"/"To Be With You"	

Wing

90008	"Two Things I Love"/"Glass Heart"	

THE DIAMONDS

The Diamonds, a Canadian vocal group, successfully transformed some rhythm and blues material into sharply executed popular rock and roll. Their biggest hit, "Little Darlin'," so far outdistanced the muddy first version by The Gladiolas, that the song is essentially a Diamonds original. This tailoring and refining of a rhythm and blues recording into an improved product is the exception to the rule. The earlier cover performance by The Diamonds of "Why Do Fools Fall In Love," though the national hit, is hardly as enduring as the original by The Teenagers, with the unique Frankie Lymon lead vocal. The same holds true for The Diamonds' covers of "Love, Love, Love," "Ka-Ding Dong," "A Thousand Miles Away" and "Silhouettes."

The original rhythm and blues performances are so satisfying, that the covers by The Diamonds seem superfluous. With the late 1957 demise of the cover record, The Diamonds adjusted to recording quality original rock and roll with "The Stroll," a 1957-58 hit; "Walking Along," a fine rock and roll version of The Solitaires original (Old Town 1034); and the novelty rocker, "She Say" in 1959.

Values

The one 45 RPM single on the Coral label is valued around $5, while issues on the original Mercury label bring from $2 to $5. "Little Darlin'" was an enormous hit, and thus is fairly easy to locate.

Discography

Coral

61502	"Black Denim Trousers and Motorcycle Boots"/"Nip Sip"	1955

Mercury

70790	"Why Do Fools Fall In Love"/"You Baby You"	1956

70835	"The Church Bells May Ring"/"Little Girl Of Mine"	
70889	"Love, Love, Love"/"Ev'ry Night About This Time"	
70934	"Ka-Ding Dong"/"Soft Summer Breeze"	
70983	"My Judge And Jury"/"Put Your House In Order"	
71021	"A Thousand Miles Away"/"Every Minute Of The Day"	
71060	"Little Darlin'"/"Faithful And True"	1957
71128	"Words Of Love"/"Don't Say Goodbye"	
71165	"Zip Zip"/"Oh, How I Wish"	
71197	"Silhouettes"/"Daddy Cool"	
71242	"The Stroll"/"Land Of Beauty"	
71291	"High Sign"/"Chick-Lets"	1958
71330	"Kathy-O"/"Happy Heart"	
71366	"Walking Along"/"Eternal Lovers"	
71404	"She Say"/"From The Bottom Of My Heart"	1959
71449	"Gretchen"/"A Mother's Love"	
71468	"Sneaky Alligator"/"Holding Your Hand"	
71505	"Young In Years"/"The Twenty Second Day"	
71534	"Walkin' The Stroll"/"Batman, Wolf-man, Frankenstein And Dracula"	
71586	"Tell The Truth"/"Real True Love"	1960
71633	"Slave Girl"/"The Pencil Song"	
71734	"You'd Be Mine"/"The Crumble"	
71818	"Woomai-Ling"/"The Munch"	1961
71831	"One Summer Night"/"It's A Doggone Shame"	

Novelty Records

◉

The rock and roll novelty record of the 50's and 60's took on several distinctive forms: the early black humor of Nervous Norvous, the monster spoofs of John "Cool Ghoul" Zacherle and Bobby "Boris" Pickett. Conversely, the electronically created Chipmunks were symbolic of complete childlike innocence. Finally, there were the unique "break-in" recordings, most successfully created by Buchanan And Goodman.

DAVID SEVILLE/THE CHIPMUNKS

The Chipmunks were the invention of David Seville, a pseudonym for the late Ross Bagdasarian. As David Seville, his first smash hit single was "Witch Doctor," a clever rock and roll creation using the same squeaky voice which reappeared as The Chipmunks. These high pitched voices were actually Seville's vocal recorded at an altered speed, giving it a childlike quality. The Chipmunks' first record was the enormous hit, "The Chipmunk Song," initially released during Christmas of 1958. It was very popular during the next several Christmases. "The Chipmunk Song" was at once the most adored and most hated recording of the 1958 holiday season; it was by far the biggest hit of that year. Follow-ups featured the rascally Alvin in the hit releases, "Alvin's Harmonica" and "Alvin For President," the latter coinciding with the 1960 presidential campaign. Seville's skillful pop-jazz arrangements graced the flip sides of these Chipmunk recordings. The Chipmunk craze quietly passed in the early 60's, yet "The Chipmunk Song" endures as a Christmas classic.

Values

The Mercury and Coral label releases by Ross Bagdasarian on 45 RPM would certainly command around $5. Later releases on Liberty, especially the fine "Witch Doctor," are in the $2 to $3 range. Singles by The Chipmunks are not in especially great demand by collectors; they never exceed $2 in value, even with a picture sleeve.

Discography

As by Ross Bagdasarian:

Coral
60597 "The Girl With The Tambourine"/"He Says 'Mm-Hmm'" 1951

Mercury
70254 "Hey Brother, Pour The Wine"/"Let's Have A Merry Merry Christmas" 1953

Liberty
55013 "The Bold And The Brave"/"See A Teardrop Fall" 1955

55619 "Lucy Lucy"/"Scallywags & Sinners"

As by David Seville:

Liberty

55041	"Armen's Theme"/"Carousel In Rome"	1956
55055	"The Donkey And The Schoolboy"/"The Gift"	
55079	"Gotta Get To Your House"/"Camel Rock"	1957
55105	"Pretty Dark Eyes"/"Cecilia"	
55113	"Starlight Starbright"/"Bagdad Express"	
55132	"Witch Doctor"/"Don't Whistle At Me Baby"	1958
55140	"The Bird On My Head"/"Hey There Moon"	
55153	"The Little Brass Band"/"Take Five"	
55163	"The Mountain"/"Mr. Grape"	
55193	"Judy"/"Maria From Madrid"	1959

As by The Chipmunks

Liberty

55168	"The Chipmunk Song"/"Almost Good" (also on Liberty 55250)	1958
55179	"Alvin's Harmonica"/"Mediocre"	1959
55200	"Ragtime Cowboy Joe"/"Flip Side"	
55233	"Alvin's Orchestra"/"Copyright 1960"	1960
55243	"Coming Round The Mountain"/"Sing A Goofy Song"	
55277	"Alvin For President"/"Sack Time"	
55289	"Rudolph The Red Nosed Reindeer"/"Spain"	
55424	"The Alvin Twist"/"I Wish I Could Speak French"	1962
55452	"America The Beautiful"/"My Wild Irish Rose"	
55632	"The Night Before Christmas"/"Eefin' Alvin"	1963

55734	"All My Lovin' "/"Do You Want to Know A Secret"	1964
55773	"Do-Re-Mi"/"Super-Califragilistic-Explialidocious"	1965
55832	"I'm Henry The VIII I Am"/"What's New Pussycat"	
56079	"The Chipmunk Song"/"Christmas Blues" (with Canned Heat)	1968
Sunset		
61003	"Chitty Chitty Bang Bang"/"Hushabye Mountain"	

NERVOUS NORVOUS

Nervous Norvous was the originator of the outrageous novelty rock and roll record. Norvous's "Transfusion" became a major smash hit because it was both macabre and funny—comedy with a rock and roll backbeat. "Transfusion" was a droll, first person narrative of a series of bloody car wrecks; in 1956 this was very effective comedy. Switching to a jungle/caveman motif, Nervous Norvous recorded "Ape Call," and much later, "Stone Age Woo," complete with caveman courtship patter. "The Fang" recounted outer space visits.

Values

Single 45 RPM releases by Nervous Norvous, classic novelty rock and roll, are now in great demand. "Transfusion," Norvous's only good seller, can still fetch $5 to $7, if on the original maroon Dot label. The other Dot issues and the Embee label single can bring around $10.

Discography

Dot

15470	"Transfusion"/"Dig"	1956
15485	"Ape Call"/"Wild Dog Of Kentucky"	
15500	"The Fang"/"Bullfrog Hop"	

Embee

117	"Stone Age Woo"/"I Like Girls"	1959

BREAK-IN RECORDS: BUCHANAN AND GOODMAN

The break-in record was also widely known as the "flying saucer" record in deference to the title of the earliest and most successful of all break-ins: Buchanan And Goodman's "Flying Saucer Pt. 1 & Pt. 2." The popularity of the break-in was derived from topicality, the subject was always of great current interest. In the mid-50's, there was enormous interest in UFOs (unidentified flying objects), often called flying saucers. Later break-ins dealt with election campaigns, space shots and parodies of popular movies and television series. The second important ingredient was the use of several word excerpts from currently popular rock and roll recordings.

The team of Buchanan And Goodman created the break-in with "Back To Earth," soon retitled "The Flying Saucer," using phrases from rhythm and blues releases of 1955 and 1956 to describe an earth visit by outer space creatures. Though later Buchanan And Goodman issues did not equal the success of "The Flying Saucer," Dickie Goodman did have a 1959 hit with "The Touchables," which was modeled on a successful TV crime series.

Values

Probably of greatest collector interest is the complete set of Buchanan And Goodman releases on the Luniverse label. These 45 RPM singles are worth $5 to $7. Other break-in recordings of unusual value include "Dear Elvis" by Audrey (Plus 104) with a $20 price tag—it is much sought after by Presley collectors—and "Frankenstein of 59" by Count Dracula (Novelty 301) which can bring some $5.

Discography

As by Buchanan And Goodman:

Luniverse

101	"Back To Earth Pt. 1 & Pt. 2" (retitled "The Flying Saucer")	1956
102	"Public Opinion" (retitled "Buchanan And Goodman On Trial"/"Crazy")	
103	"The Banana Boat Story"/"The Mystery"	
105	"Flying Saucer The 2nd"/"Martian Melody"	
107	"Santa And The Satellite Pt. 1 & Pt. 2"	
108	"The Flying Saucer Goes West"/ "Saucer Serenade"	1957

Comedy

500	"Flying Saucer The 3rd"/"The Cha Cha Lesson"	

As by Count Dracula:

Novelty

301	"Frankenstein Of '59"/"Frankenstein Returns"	1959

As by Dickie Goodman:

Mark X

8009	"The Touchables"/"Martian Melody"	

8010 "The Touchables In Brooklyn"/"Mystery"

JOHN ZACHERLE

At first dubbed "The Cool Ghoul," John Zacherle created a grisly rock and roll classic, "Dinner With Drac." This tale, which recounted a vividly gory dinner menu with ghastly detail, developed into a major 1957 hit.

Values

John Zacherle's early Cameo label efforts can bring about $5, while later issues are worth some $2.

Discography

Cameo

130	"Dinner With Drac Pt. 1 & Pt. 2"	1957
139	"Lunch With Mother Goose"/"Eight Two Tombstones"	

Parkway

853	"Dinner With Drac"/"Hurry Bury Baby"	1962

Colpix

743	"Monsters Have Problems Too"/"Hello Dolly"	1965

THE HOLLYWOOD ARGYLES

A Los Angeles rock and roll combo, The Hollywood Argyles achieved immediate number one hit status with "Alley-Oop," a droll spoken novelty performance with a clanging rock and roll backbeat. Other novelty 45 RPM singles by The Argyles, including

"Gun Totin' Critter Named Jack" and "You've Been Torturing Me"—taken from the original by The Four Young Men (Crest 1076)—made use of a similar easy-going rock and roll beat.

Values

Single 45 RPM recordings by The Hollywood Argyles on Lute and Paxley command from $2 to $3.

Discography

Lute

5905 "Alley-Oop"/"Sho Know A Lot About Love" 1960

5908 "Gun Totin' Critter Named Jack"/"The Bug Eyed Man"

6002 "Hully Gully"/"So Fine"

As by Gary Paxton And The Hollywood Argyles:

Paxley

752 "You've Been Torturing Me"/"The Grubble" 1961

As by The Hollywood Argyles:

Chatahoochie

691 "Long-Hair-Unsquare Dude Called Jack"/"Ole" 1965

As by The New Hollywood Argyles:

Kammy

105 "Alley Oop '66"/"Do The Funky Foot" 1966

LARRY VERNE

Larry Verne, a specialist in the low-key comedy monologue, portrayed the long-suffering innocent caught in stormy, troubled circumstances. Verne's first and by far biggest hit was "Mr. Custer," in which he begged the ill-fated general not to take him into battle. Verne's performance was supplemented with an Indian war chant backing.

Values

The value of Larry Verne 45 RPM singles is a firm $2.

Discography

Era

3024	"Mr. Custer"/"Okeefenokee Two Step"	1960
3034	"Mr. Livingston"/"Roller Coaster"	
3044	"Tubby Tilly"/"Abdul's Party"	1961
3051	"Charlie At The Bat"/"Pow Right In The Kisser"	
3065	"Beatnick"/"The Speck"	
3075	"I'm A Brave Little Soldier"/"Hoo-Ha"	1962
3091	"The Coward That Won The West"	

BOBBY "BORIS" PICKETT

Bobby "Boris" Pickett skillfully combined the monster lyric with the type of dance beat so popular in the early 60's twist era into the major hit "Monster Mash." This record was popular in 1962, then became a repeat top ten hit record in 1974. Later issues by Pickett continued this rockin' and rollin' monster theme.

Values

Original Garpax label 45's by Bobby Pickett bring around $2.

Discography

Garpax

44167	"Monster Mash"/"Monster's Mash Party"	1962
44171	"Monster's Holiday"/"Monster Motion"	
44175	"Graduation Day"/"The Humpty Dumpty"	
44185	"Me And My Mummy"	

RCA

8312	"Smoke Smoke That Cigarette"/"Gotta Leave This Town"	
8459	"The Monster Swim"/"The Werewolf Watusi"	1964

Rockabilly Roots

⊙

Mid-50's rock and roll was the era of giants: Fats Domino, Little Richard and Chuck Berry were doing blues-based rock and roll, while white rockabilly and rock and roll was dominated by Bill Haley And The Comets, Elvis Presley, Gene Vincent And The Blue-caps, Carl Perkins and Buddy Holly And The Crickets. Other rock and roll artists popular during this period had a similar rockabilly background, yet opted for a softer, more teen-oriented rock and roll style. This pop approach, in turn, influenced the later sound of more mainstream rock and roll artists.

THE EVERLY BROTHERS

The recording career of The Everly Brothers began with a little-noted issue on the Columbia label country and western series. The Everlys' next recordings were on the Cadence label, and these efforts met with entirely different and more profitable results.

"Bye Bye Love" and "Wake Up Little Susie"

brought The Everly Brothers instant success. Both recordings developed into two of the major hits of 1957. "Bye Bye Love" and "Wake Up Little Susie" were both engaging rockers, as was the biting "Bird Dog" in 1958. In contrast, "All I Have To Do Is Dream" and "Devoted To You" were appealing, countrified love ballads. Most of the best material by The Everly Brothers possessed a solid rock and roll beat, including the consistently good sellers "Problems" and "Poor Jenny." "Cathy's Clown," the initial Warner Brothers offering, was an immediate hit, as were such follow-ups, the melancholy "Ebony Eyes" and "So Sad." By the mid- and later 60's, The Everly Brothers experienced sharply declining record sales. Some later issues, including "The Price Of Love," were commercial flops, yet they were excellent performances.

Values

The Everly Brothers' Columbia label single is sought after by rockabilly collectors; on 45 RPM they can command from $8 to $10. Cadence and Warner Brothers label issues are fairly easy to locate. They fetch up to $3 with a picture sleeve, and up to $2 without a picture sleeve.

Discography

Columbia

21496	"Keep A 'Lovin' Me"/"The Sun Keeps Shining"	1955

Cadence

1315	"Bye Bye Love"/"I Wonder If I Care Too Much"	1957
1337	"Wake Up Little Susie"/"Maybe Tomorrow"	

1342 "This Little Girl Of Mine"/"Should We Tell Him"
1348 "All I Have To Do Is Dream"/"Claudette" 1958
1350 "Bird Dog"/"Devoted To You"
1355 "Problems"/"Love Of My Life"
1364 "Poor Jenny"/"Take A Message To Mary" 1959
1369 "(Til) I Kissed You"/"Oh What A Feeling"
1376 "Let It Be Me"/"Since You Broke My Heart"
1380 "Be Bop A Lula"/"When Will I Be Loved" 1960
1388 "Like Strangers"/"Brand New Heartache"
1429 "I'm Here To Get My Baby Out Of Jail"/"Lightning Express" 1962

Warner Brothers
5151 "Cathy's Clown"/"Always It's You" 1960
5163 "So Sad"/"Lucille"
5199 "Ebony Eyes"/"Walk Right Back" 1961
5220 "Temptation"/"Stick With Me Baby"
5250 "Crying In The Rain"/"I'm Not Angry" 1962
5273 "That's Old Fashioned"/"How Can I Meet Her"
5297 "No One Can Make My Sunshine Smile"/"Don't Ask Me To Be Friends"
5346 "So It Will Always Be"/"Nancy's Minuet" 1963
5362 "It's Been Nice"/"I'm Afraid"
5389 "The Girl Sang The Blues"/"Love Her"
5422 "Ain't That Lovin' You Baby"/"Hello Amy"
5441 "The Ferris Wheel"/"Don't Forget To Cry" 1964
5478 "Gone Gone Gone"/"Torture"
5501 "Don't Blame Me"/"Muskrat"
5600 "You're My Girl"/"Don't Let The Whole World Know" 1965
5611 "That'll Be The Day"/"Give Me A Sweetheart"
5628 "The Price Of Love"
5649 "Love Is Strange"/"Man With Money"
5682 "It's All Over"/"I Used To Love You"

5698 "The Doll House Is Empty"/"Lovely Kravezit" 1966
5808 "Power Of Love"/"Leave My Girl Alone"
5833 "Somebody Help Me"/"Hard Hard Years"
5857 "Like Everything Before"/"Fifi The Flea"
5901 "Devils Child"/"Never Smiles"
7020 "Bowling Green"/"I Don't Want To Love You"
7121 "All I Have To Do Is Dream"/"Bye Bye Love"
7192 "Empty Boxes"/"It's My Time"
7290 "I'm On My Way Home Again"

GEORGE HAMILTON IV

George Hamilton's forte was the rockabilly love ballad, unique in the mid-50's, which was saturated with rock and roll. Hamilton's first release was the appealing expression of adolescent love, "A Rose And A Baby Ruth." Originally issued by the small Southern-based Colonial label, "A Rose And A Baby Ruth" became a major 1956 hit only after reissuance on the larger ABC label. George Hamilton's "Why Don't They Understand" was the definitive statement of the 50's generation gap. "Why Don't They Understand" was the predecessor for a vast range of material with a similar theme.

Values

The original Colonial label recording of "A Rose And A Baby Ruth" is worth about $10, while the ABC reissue and later releases are in the $3 range.

Discography

Colonial
420 "A Rose And A Baby Ruth"/"If You Don't Know" 1956

ABC

9765	"A Rose And A Baby Ruth"/"If You Don't Know"	1956
9782	"If I Possessed A Printing Press"/"Only One Love"	1957
9838	"High School Romance"/"Everybody's Body"	
9862	"Why Don't They Understand"/"Even Tho"	
9898	"Now And For Always"/"One Heart"	1958
9924	"I Know Where I'm Goin'"/"Who's Taking You To The Prom"	
9946	"Your Cheatin' Heart"/"When Will I Know"	
9966	"The Two Of Us"/"Lucy Lucy"	
10009	"The Steady Game"/"Can You Blame Us"	1959
10028	"Gee"/"I Know Your Sweetheart"	
10123	"Before This Day Ends"/"Loneliness All Around"	1960
10167	"It's Just The Idea"/"A Walk On The Wild Side Of Life"	

BOBBY HELMS

Bobby Helms used a relaxed, slightly discordant vocal delivery in his initial fine rockabilly hit, "My Special Angel." Helms's next success, "Jingle Bell Rock," featured a stronger uptempo vocal. It has since become a rock and roll Christmas classic.

Values

Bobby Helms's first single "Tennessee Rock And Roll" is rare on 45 RPM and can bring up to $5. Releases after the success of "My Special Angel" are not as scarce, bringing $2 to $3.

Discography

Decca

29947	"Tennessee Rock And Roll"/"I Don't Owe You Nothing"	1956
30194	"Fraulein"/"Heartsick Feeling"	1957
30423	"My Special Angel"/"Standing At The End Of The World"	
30513	"Jingle Bell Rock"/"Captain Santa Claus"	
30557	"Just A Little Lonesome"/"Love My Lady"	1958
30619	"Jacqueline"/"Living In The Shadow Of The Past"	
30682	"Schoolboy Crush"/"Borrowed Dreams"	
30749	"The Fool And The Angel"/"A Hundred Hearts"	
30831	"New River Train"/"Miss Memory"	1959
30886	"I Guess I'll Miss The Prom"/"Soon It Can Be Told"	
30976	"Hurry Baby"/"My Lucky Day"	
31041	"To My Sorrow"/"Someone Was Already There"	

BRENDA LEE

Only nine years of age at the beginning of her recording career, "Little" Brenda Lee belted out a fine number of rollicking rock and roll singles on the Decca label. Several of her earliest efforts, including "Bigelow 6-200," "Dynamite" and "Rockin' Around The Christmas Tree," though now minor rock classics, were not impressive hits at the point of first release. Brenda Lee's first major hit was the 1959 success, "Sweet Nothin's." Her hit string continued with several ballads, "I'm Sorry," "I Want To Be Wanted" and "Emotions," all nicely done in Brenda Lee's unique little-girl voice. Brenda Lee was among a handful of brilliant female rock and roll artists of the late 50's and early 60's.

Values

Brenda Lee's solitary Apollo label release, as well as her first eight Decca singles, are now somewhat scarce on 45 RPM. The better Decca label rockabilly performances, especially "Bigelow 6-200," "Dynamite" and "Rock The Bop," are in demand; they can bring $5 to $8. Later singles after the hit "Sweet Nothin's" are less rare and are worth around $2.

Discography

As by Brenda Lee:

Apollo

490	"Ain't Gonna Give Nobody None"/"If I Ever Get Rich"	1956

As by Little Brenda Lee (9 years old):

Decca

30050	"Bigelow 6-200"/"Jambalaya"	

As by Brenda Lee:

Decca

30107	"Christy Christmas"/"I'm Gonna Lasso Santa Claus"	
30198	"One Step At A Time"/"Fairlyland"	1957
30333	"Dynamite"/"Love You Till I Die"	
30411	"Ain't That Love"/"One Teenager To Another"	
30535	"Rock The Bop"/"Rock-A-Bye Baby Blues"	1958
30673	"Ring A My Phone"/"Little Jonah"	
30776	"Rockin' Around The Christmas Tree"/"Papa Noel"	
30885	"Let's Jump The Broomstick"/"Some Of These Days"	1959

30967	"Sweet Nothin's"/"Weep No More My Baby"	
31093	"I'm Sorry"/"That's All You Gotta Do"	1960
31149	"I Want To Be Wanted"/"Just A Little"	
31195	"Emotions"/"I'm Learning About Love"	
31231	"You Can Depend On Me"/"It's Never Too Late"	1961
31272	"Dum Dum"/"Eventually"	
31309	"Fool #1"/"Anybody But Me"	
31348	"Break It To Me Gently"/"So Deep"	1962
31379	"Here Comes That Feeling"/"Everybody Loves Me But You"	
31407	"Heart In Hand"/"It Started All Over Again"	
31424	"All Alone Am I"/"Save All Your Lovin" For Me"	
31454	"Your Used To Be"/"She'll Never Know"	
31478	"Losing You"/"He's So Heavenly"	1963
31510	"I Wonder"/"My Whole World Is Falling Down"	
31539	"The Grass Is Greener"/"Sweet Impossible You"	
31570	"As Usual"/"Lonely Lonely Lonely Me"	
31599	"Think"/"The Waiting Game"	1964
31628	"Alone With You"/"My Dreams"	
31654	"When You Loved Me"/"He's Sure To Remember Me"	
31687	"Jingle Bell Rock"/"Winter Wonderland"	
31690	"Is It True"/"Just Behind The Rainbow"	
31728	"The Crying Game"/"Thanks A Lot"	1965
31762	"I Still Miss Someone"/"Truly Truly True"	
31792	"No One"/"Too Many Rivers"	
31849	"Rusty Bells"/"If You Don't"	

JIMMY BOWEN/BUDDY KNOX

The recording careers of Jimmy Bowen and Buddy Knox began in an unusually linked fashion. The first hit song of each—Bowen's "I'm Stickin' With You Baby" and Knox's "Party Doll"—initially appeared on the same Triple D 45 RPM single. Both of these early titles were re-released individually on the infant Roulette label. Bowen's relaxed approach to rockabilly was evident in his series of pop-tempo singles, which were done in a soft Pat Boone style.

Buddy Knox recordings are more strongly rhythmic, as is apparent in his classic hit, the soft bopper "Party Doll." "Party Doll" is an example of the reverse cover record in that Knox, a white rockabilly artist had the song covered by rhythm and blues artist Roy Brown. Knox's rock and roll style was successful with such mild hits as "Rock Your Little Baby To Sleep" in 1957 and the rougher "Somebody Touched Me" in 1958.

Values

The Triple D original which featured both Bowen and Knox is a prime rockabilly collector's treasure, commanding $10 to $15. The Roulette reissues, Roulette 4001 by Bowen and Roulette 4002 by Knox, along with later Roulette 45 RPM singles by either artist, are generally worth about $3.

JIMMY BOWEN

Discography

Triple D

797	"I'm Stickin' With You Baby"/ "Party Doll" (by Buddy Knox)	1957

Roulette

4001	"I'm Stickin' With You Baby"/"Ever Lovin' Fingers"	1957
4010	"I Trusted You"/"Warm Up To Me Baby"	
4017	"Ever Since That Night"/"Don't Tell Me Your Troubles"	

4023	"Cross Over"/"It's Shameful"	
4083	"By The Light Of The Silvery Moon"/ "The Two Step"	1958
4102	"My Kind Of Woman"/"Blue Moon"	
4122	"Always Faithful"/"Wish I Were Tied To You"	1959
4175	"You're Just Wasting Your Time"/ "Walkin' On Air"	
4224	"Oh Yeah Oh Yeah Mm Mm"/"Your Loving Arms"	

Crest

1085	"Don't Drop It"/"Somebody To Love"	1961

BUDDY KNOX AND THE RHYTHM ORCHIDS

Discography

Triple D

797	"Party Doll"/"I'm Stickin' With You Baby" (Jimmy Bowen)	1957

Roulette

4002	"Party Doll"/"My Baby's Gone"	1957
4009	"Rock Your Little Baby To Sleep"/"Don't Make Me Cry" (by Lieutenant Buddy Knox)	
4018	"Devil Woman"/"Hula Love"	
4042	"Swingin' Daddy"/"Whenever I'm Lonely"	1958
4082	"Somebody Touched Me"/"C'mon Baby"	
4120	"That's Why I Cry"/"Teasable Pleasable You"	1959
4140	"Think I'm Gonna Kill Myself"/"To Be With You"	
4179	"Taste Of The Blues"/"I Ain't Sharin' Sharon"	
4262	"Long Lonely Nights"/"Storm Clouds"	1960

Liberty

55290	"Lovey Dovey"/"I Got You"	1960
55305	"Ling Ting Tong"/"The Kisses"	1961
55366	"All By Myself"/"Three Eyed Man"	
55411	"Chi-Hua-Hua"/"Open"	1962
55473	"She's Gone"/"Now There's Only Me"	
55503	"Dear Abby"/"Three Way Love Affair"	
55592	"Tomorrow Is A Comin'"/"Shadaroom"	1963
55650	"Thanks A Lot"/"Hitchhike Back To Georgia"	

Ruff

101	"Jo-Ann"/"Don't Make A Ripple" (also on RRG 1001)	1965

Reprise

0395	"Good Time Girl"/"Livin' In A House Full Of Love"	1965
0431	"A Lover's Question"/"You Said Goodbye"	
0463	"A White Sport Coat"/"That Don't Do Me No Good"	

United Artists

50301	"Gypsy Man"/"This Time Tomorrow"	1968
50463	"A Million Years Or So"/"Tonight My Sleepless Night Is Coming Back To Town"	

Early Teen Idols

Elvis Presley was the dominant rock and roll performer of the mid- and late 50's. Presley's enormous fan appeal gave impetus to slightly lesser, yet just as intense, fan devotion to several other attractive, young rock and roll idols. Both Paul Anka and the late Bobby Darin had previous releases before scoring a major hit, but when they did have a hit record it was in a very big way.

Ricky Nelson's appeal was of the instant hit record variety. Teenagers of the 50's had known Ricky Nelson from childhood, they grew up with him through the weekly "Ozzie And Harriet" radio and television series. Billed in his pre-recording years as "the irrepressible Ricky," he came across as an extremely likable teenager. When Ricky began singing on the series, his fans were ready for and accepting of his pouting rock and roll. Success was, in part, a happy accident in that it paved the way for rock and roll releases by other youthful television and movie stars.

PAUL ANKA

In 1956, Paul Anka was featured on a little-known RPM label release, "I Confess," which was recorded with The Jacks, a popular rhythm and blues vocal group. "I Confess" was not successful. However, in 1957 the record "Diana" proved to be an immediate smash hit for the teenage Paul Anka. "Diana" was a vigorous, flashy rock and roll performance. The lyric concerned an infatuation with an older lover and apparently reached a very receptive audience.

With few exceptions, Paul Anka succeeded with self-composed material that gave him a long string of romantic hits noted for their lush production. The dramatic "You Are My Destiny" was a major 1958 hit. This powerful ballad was a forerunner in style for later best sellers including "My Heart Sings" in 1958, "I Miss You So" and "Put Your Head On My Shoulder" in 1959 and "Puppy Love" in 1960. Another 1959 single by Paul Anka was the throbbing "Lonely Boy," a rock and roll classic possessing enormous intensity.

By the early 60's, single releases by Paul Anka, though no longer major hits, continued to sell consistently well. By the very late 60's, Paul Anka's career was temporarily diverted away from the single rock and roll release and toward such middle of the road hits as "My Way." As late as 1974, Anka returned with a major rock and roll hit, "You're Having My Baby."

Values

Paul Anka's first record, the little-known RPM label 45 RPM single, is worth $15 to $20. The earliest of the ABC label issues (to ABC 9974)—along with the obscure "It's Christmas Everywhere"—can bring $3 or $4, while later ABC label singles fetch about $2.

Discography

RPM

472	"I Confess"/"Blau-Wile Deveest Fontaine"	1956

ABC

9831	"Diana"/"Don't Gamble With Love"	1957
9880	"You Are My Destiny"/"When I Stop Loving You"	1958
9907	"Crazy Love"/"Let The Bells Keep Ringing"	
9937	"Midnight"/"Verboten!"	
9956	"Just Young"/"So It's Goodbye"	
9974	"The Teen Commandments"/"If You Learn To Pray" (with Johnny Nash and George Hamilton IV)	
9987	"My Heart Sings"/"That's Love"	
10011	"I Miss You So"/"Late Last Night"	1959
10022	"Lonely Boy"/"Your Way"	
10040	"Put Your Head On My Shoulder"/"Don't Ever Leave Me"	
10064	"It's Time To Cry"/"Something Has Changed Me"	
10083	"Puppy Love"/"Adam And Eve"	1960
10106	"My Home Town"/"Something Happened"	
10132	"Hello Young Lovers"/"I Love You In The Same Old Way"	
10147	"Summer's Gone"/"I'd Have To Share"	1960
10168	"The Story Of My Love"/"Don't Say You're Sorry"	
10169	"It's Christmas Everywhere"/"Rudolph The Red-Nosed Reindeer"	
10194	"Tonight My Love Tonight"/"I'm Just Your Fool Anyway"	1961
10220	"Dance On Little Girl"/"I Talk To You"	
10239	"Cinderella"/"Kissin' On The Phone"	
10279	"Loveland"/"The Bells At My Wedding"	
10282	"The Fools Hall Of Fame"/"Far From The Lights Of Town"	

… Find Another You"/"Uh Huh"

… ing Home"/"Cry"

… Warm And Tender"/"I'd Like
… ow" 1961

… Guitar And A Glass Of Wine"/
"I Never Knew Your Name" 1962

8068 "Every Night"/"There You Go"

8097 "Eso Beso"/"Give Me Back My Heart"

8115 "Crying In The Wind"/"Love"

8170 "Remember Diana"/"At Night" 1963

8195 "Hello Jim"/"You've Got The Nerve To Call This Love"

8237 "Wondrous Are The Ways Of Love"/ "Hurry Up And Tell Me"

8272 "Did You Have A Happy Birthday"/"For No Good Reason At All"

8311 "From Rocking Horse To Rocking Chair"/ "Cheer Up"

8396 "It's Easy To Say"/"In My Imagination" 1964

8493 "Sylvia"/"Behind My Smile"

8595 "The Loneliest Boy In The World"/ "Dream Me Happy" 1965

8662 "As If There Were No Tomorrow"/ "Every Day A Heart Is Broken"

8764 "Oh, Such A Stranger"/"Truly Yours" 1966

8839 "I Wish"/"I Went To Your Wedding"

8893 "Can't Get Along Very Well Without Her"/ "I Can't Help Loving You"

9032 "I'd Rather Be A Stranger"/"Poor Old Fool"

9457 "Can't Get You Out Of My Mind"/"When We Get There"

9612 "But For Love"/"The Boy With Green Eyes" 1967

9648 "Goodnight My Love"/"This Crazy World" 1968

9767 "Happy"/"Can't Get You Out Of My Mind" 1969

846 "Midnight Mistress"/"Before It's Too Late—This Land Is Your Land"

BOBBY DARIN

The late Bobby Darin originally recorded several folk-styled ballads for Decca Records. Of these Decca singles, the best known is the moderate seller "Rock Island Line," together with "Blue Eyed Mermaid," which was influenced by Frankie Laine. Darin opted for a solidly successful rock and roll format when he switched to the Atco label. His "Splish Splash" was a fine novelty rocker and along with follow-ups by The Rinky Dinks "Early In The Morning" and "Mighty Mighty Man," Darin came across with some strong rocking performances. The steady-beat "Queen Of The Hop" and the sparkling "Dream Lover" were both ideal rock and roll vehicles for Bobby Darin.

"Mack The Knife," by far his biggest hit, marked a radical turning point for Darin. From early 1958 to mid-1959, Bobby Darin met with considerable success doing teen beat rock and roll and producing several classics. However, with the release of "Mack The Knife," Darin gave evidence that his primary goal was to achieve status as a popular middle-of-the-road performer. "Mack The Knife" was such a pop-styled release and was an impressive success. Bobby Darin attempted to match this hit with substantially weaker pop material but was unable to record a major follow-up hit. Toward the mid-60's Bobby Darin experimented with various changes in style. Bobby Darin turned to serious composition—just as Paul Anka did—which is exemplified by the poetic "If I Were A Carpenter."

Values

The poor selling Bobby Darin singles on the Decca label can bring from $5 to $7 on 45 RPM. The earliest Atco singles (to Atco 6121) are worth $3 or slightly more, while subsequent issues bring about $2.

Discography

Bobby Darin And The Jaybirds:

Decca

29883	"Rock Island Line"/"Timber"	1956
29922	"Silly Willy"/"Blue Eyed Mermaid"	
30031	"The Greatest Builder"/"Hear Them Bells"	
30225	"Dealer In Dreams"/"Help Me"	1957

As by The Rinky Dinks:

Atco

6121	"Early In The Morning"/"Now We're One"	1958
6128	"Mighty Mighty Man"/"You're Mine"	

As by Bobby Darin:

Atco

6092	"I Found A Million Dollar Baby"/"Talk To Me"	1957
6103	"Don't Call My Name"/"Pretty Baby"	
6109	"Just In Case You Change Your Mind"/"So Mean"	
6117	"Splish Splash"/"Judy, Don't Be Moody"	1958
6127	"Queen Of The Hop"/"Lost Love"	
6133	"Plain Jane"/"When I'm Gone"	
6140	"Dream Lover"/"Bullmoose"	1959
6147	"Mack The Knife"/"Was There A Call For Me"	
6158	"Beyond The Sea"/"That's The Way Love Is"	
6161	"Tall Story"/"Clementine"	1960

6167	"Won't You Come Home Bill Bailey"/ "I'll Be There"	
6173	"Beachcomber"/"Autumn Blues" (instrumental)	
6179	"Artificial Flowers"/"Somebody To Love"	
6183	"Child Of God"/"Christmas Auld Lang Syne"	
6188	"Lazy River"/"Oo-Ee-Train"	1961
6196	"Nature Boy"/"Look For My True Love"	
6200	"Come September"/"Walk Back To Me"	
6206	"You Must Have Been A Beautiful Baby"/ "Sorrow Tomorrow"	
6211	"O Come All Ye Faithful"/"Ave Maria"	
6214	"Multiplication"/"Irresistible You"	1962
6221	"What'd I Say Pt. 1 & Pt. 2"	
6229	"Things"/"Jailer Bring Me Water"	
6236	"Baby Face"/"You Know How"	1963

RICKY NELSON

The worldwide exposure of Ricky Nelson in the television series "Ozzie And Harriet" ensured that Nelson would emerge as one of the first rock and roll superstars to have his career shaped by media influence. Ricky Nelson's earliest recording was "I'm Walkin'," a rhythm and blues composition and arrangement borrowed from Fats Domino. The flip side, "A Teenager's Romance," and the next release "You're My One And Only Love" were both teenage love ballads; each achieved moderate hit status.

The first smash hits for Ricky Nelson were rendered in the classic rock and roll idiom. "Be Bop Baby," "Stood Up" and "My Bucket's Got A Hole In It" were each nationally best selling singles. Both "My Bucket's Got A Hole In It" and "Waitin' In School" were surprisingly fine rockabilly performances, each neatly embellished with skillful stomping guitar work by the renowned Burnette Brothers

—Johnny and Dorsey. "Poor Little Fool" and "Lonesome Town" are contrastingly downbeat, somewhat melancholy ballads, each touching upon an important late 50's pop rock and roll theme of exaggerated self-pity.

"I Got A Feeling" and "It's Late" were irresistible rock and roll performances, similar in effect to Ricky Nelson's earliest and best rock and roll records. Ricky Nelson's early 60's releases were consistently good sellers, though his career was entering a slow decline. Hits of the 60's included the syrupy "Young Emotions," the chauvinistic "Travelin' Man" and the plaintive "Teenage Idol." "Teenage Idol" was a predecessor to Nelson's hit of the 70's, "Garden Party," both variations of the theme that it sure enough is tough to be a popular rock and roll star.

Values

Ricky Nelson recorded two Verve label singles, "You're My One And Only Love" on 45 RPM is the rarest, and can bring over $5. "I'm Walkin'," a better seller, is worth $3 to $5. On the original label, and with picture sleeves, Nelson's earliest Imperial label singles (to Imperial 5528) can bring up to $5, while later issues are worth about $2.

Discography

As by Ricky Nelson:

Verve

10047	"A Teenager's Romance"/"I'm Walkin'"	1957
10070	"You're My One And Only Love"/"Honey Rock" (instrumental by Barney Kessell)	

Imperial

5463	"Be Bop Baby"/"Have I Told You Lately That I Love You"	1957
5483	"Stood Up"/"Waitin' In School"	
5503	"My Bucket's Got A Hole In It"/"Believe What You Say"	1958
5528	"Poor Little Fool"/"Don't Leave Me This Way"	
5545	"I Got A Feeling"/"Lonesome Town"	
5565	"It's Late"/"Never Be Anyone Else But You"	1959
5595	"Sweeter Than You"/"Just A Little Too Much"	
5614	"I Wanna Be Loved"/"Mighty Good"	
5663	"Young Emotions"/"Right By My Side"	1960
5685	"Yes Sir, That's My Baby"/"I'm Not Afraid"	
5707	"You Are The Only One"/"Milk Cow Blues"	1961
5741	"Hello Mary Lou"/"Travelin' Man"	
5770	"A Wonder Like You"/"Everlovin'"	
5805	"Young World"/"Summertime"	1962
5864	"Teenage Idol"/"I've Got My Eyes On You"	

As by Rick Nelson:

Imperial

5901	"It's Up To You"/"I Need You"	
5910	"I'm In Love Again"/"That's All"	1963
5935	"If You Can't Rock Me"/"Old Enough To Love"	
5958	"A Long Vacation"/"Mad Mad World"	
5985	"Time After Time"/"There's Not A Minute"	1964
66004	"Today's Teardrops"/"Thank You Darlin'"	
66017	"Congratulations"/"One Minute To Love"	

66039 "Everybody But Me"/"Lucky Star"

Decca

31475	"I Got A Woman"/"You Don't Love Me Anymore"	1963
31495	"String Along"/"Gypsy Woman"	
31535	"Fools Rush In"/"Down Home"	
31574	"For You"/"That's All She Wrote"	
31612	"I Wonder If Your Love Will Ever Belong To Me"/"The Very Thought Of You"	1964
31656	"There's Nothing I Can Say"/"Lonely Corner"	
31703	"A Happy Guy"/"Don't Breathe A Word"	
31756	"Mean Old World"/"When The Chips Are Down"	1965

Movie Star Rock and Roll

◉

Several well-known movie and television personalities with proven strong teen appeal attempted to cash in on recording stardom. Success for these personalities was limited. Each had one or two hits at best.

TOMMY SANDS

Tommy Sands recorded the very successful ballad "Teenage Crush," a top seller of 1957. Several of Sands's follow-up releases, including one recording with Annette, were as good as "Teenage Crush," yet none became a major hit.

Values

Tommy Sands's 45 RPM singles can bring $2; if they have a picture sleeve, the value is about $3.

Discography

Capitol

3639	"Teenage Crush"/"Hep Dee Hootie"	1957
3690	"Ring-A-Ding-A-Ding"/"My Love Song"	
3723	"Goin' Steady"/"Ring My Phone"	
3743	"Let Me Be Loved"/"Fantastically Foolish"	
3810	"A Swingin' Romance"/"Man, Like Wow!"	
3867	"Sing Boy Sing"/"Crazy Cause I Love You"	1958
3953	"Teen Age Doll"/"Hawaiian Rock"	
3985	"After The Senior Prom"/"Big Date"	
4036	"Blue Ribbon Baby"/"I Love You Because"	
4082	"Bigger Than Texas"/"The Worryin' Kind"	
4160	"Is It Ever Gonna Happen"/"I Aint Gettin' Rid Of You"	1959
4259	"I'll Be Seeing You"/"That's The Way I Am"	
4405	"The Old Oaken Bucket"/"These Are The Things You Are"	1960

TAB HUNTER

Tab Hunter had one strong hit, his 1957 remake of Sonny James's "Young Love." Further issues by Hunter on the Dot label were not even near misses.

Values

Tab Hunter's 45 RPM singles on the Dot label are generally worth $2 or less.

Discography

Dot

15533	"Young Love"/"Red Sails In The Sunset"	1957

15548	"Ninety Nine Ways"/"Don't Get Around Much Anymore"	
15657	"I'm Alone Because I Love You"/"Don't Get Around Much Anymore"	
15767	"I'm A Runaway"/"It's All Over Town"	1958
16264	"You Cheated"/"The Way You Look Tonight"	1961

SAL MINEO

Sal Mineo's attempts at recording a hit record met with surprising success. His first release, "Start Movin'," a pleasant upbeat vocal was a hit. "Little Pigeon," rendered in rock and roll tempo, was a minor 1958 hit.

Values

Singles by Sal Mineo on the Epic label are worth about $2 on 45 RPM, and around $3 with a picture sleeve.

Discography

Epic

9216	"Start Movin'"/"Love Affair"	1957
9227	"Lasting Love"/"You Shouldn't Do That"	
9246	"Party Time"/"The Words That I Whisper"	
9260	"Little Pigeon"/"Cuttin' In"	1958
9271	"Seven Steps To Love"	
9327	"Young As We Are"/"Make Believe Baby"	

EDD "KOOKIE" BYRNES

Edd "Kookie" Byrnes used his hair-combing trademark from the hit TV series, "77 Sunset Strip," to full advantage in his recording career with "Kookie Kookie (Lend Me Your Comb)"—a duet with Connie Stevens. Follow-up releases also leaned heavily on Byrne's teenage jive talk, providing moderate sales to "Like I Love You."

Values

Recordings by Edd "Kookie" Byrnes on 45 RPM generally are worth $2, with a picture sleeve they fetch $3.

Discography

Warner Brothers

5047	"Kookie Kookie (Lend Me Your Comb)"/ "You're The Top"	1959
5087	"Like I Love You"/"Kookie's Mad Pad"	
5114	"Kookie's Love Song"	
5121	"Yulesville"/"Lonely Christmas"	

Rock and Roll Vocal Groups

⦿

Throughout the 50's and 60's, rock and roll group harmony maintained consistent popularity in the New York and Philadelphia metropolitan area. More often than not, these vocal groups were either Black or Puerto Rican, occasionally they were mixed. By the very late 50's, the white vocal group, often from Italian extraction, emerged from this background with strong national impact.

Danny And The Juniors, a Philadelphia vocal group, was the first to score hit success with the late 1957 and early 1958 rock and roll release "At The Hop." The popularity of Danny And The Juniors, Dion And The Belmonts, The Four Seasons, and The Royal Teens along with several other groups, extended from 1958 through the very early 1960's. Two West Coast vocal groups, The Teddy Bears from Los Angeles and The Fleetwoods from Washington State—both trios with a male lead and two female background vocalists—gave rock and roll group harmony a sound noticeably softer and sweeter than their East Coast counterparts.

THE FOUR LOVERS/THE FOUR SEASONS

The Four Lovers were about the first of many white rhythm and blues vocal groups. "The Girl In My Dreams" was recorded in 1956. The group specialized in the romantic ballad; their unique cover versions of rhythm and blues standards such as "Honey Love" and "Shake A Hand" were regional hits only.

As The Four Seasons, the group recorded an early 60's smash hit entitled "Sherry." With "Sherry," The Four Seasons became the most successful rock and roll vocal group of the year. "Sherry" was a crisply produced, high-pitched dance tempo vocal, a rock and roll sound that characterized later Vee Jay label issues by The Four Seasons. Other rock and roll hits, "Big Girls Don't Cry" and "Walk Like A Man" were interspersed with such oldie classics as "Goodnight My Love," "Long Lonely Nights" and "Sincerely." With the label switch to Phillips, The Four Seasons adopted a softer pop rock sound.

Values

The RCA 45 RPM singles by The Four Lovers are worth $7 to $10. Early material by The Four Seasons on the Gone label can bring $10, while the Alanna singles are worth about $5. The Vee Jay singles generally command $3, the Phillips releases $2 or $3.

Discography

As by The Four Lovers:

RCA

6518 "The Girl In My Dreams"/"You're The Apple Of My Eye" 1956

6519 "Honey Love"/"Please Don't Leave Me"
6646 "Be Lovey Dovey"/"Jambalaya"
6768 "Happy Am I"/"Never Never"
6812 "Shake A Hand"/"The Stranger" 1957

Epic
9255 "My Life For Your Love"/"Pucker Up"

As by Frankie Valli And The Romans:

Cindy
3012 "Come Si Bella"/"Real" 1958

As by The Four Seasons:

Gone
5122 "Bermuda"/"Spanish Lace" 1960

Alanna
555 "Don't Sweat It Baby"/"That's The Way The Ball Bounces"
558 "Love Knows No Season"/"Hot Water Bottle"

Vee Jay
456 "Sherry"/"I've Cried Before" 1962
465 "Big Girls Don't Cry"/"Connie O"
478 "Santa Claus Is Coming To Town"/"Christmas Tears"
485 "Walk Like A Man"/"Lucky Ladybug" 1963
512 "Ain't That A Shame"/"Soon"
539 "Candy Girl"/"Marlena"
562 "New Mexican Rose"/"That's The Only Way"
576 "Peanuts"/"Stay"
582 "Goodnight My Love"/"Stay" 1964
597 "Long Lonely Nights"/"Alone"
608 "Sincerely"/"One Song"
618 "Happy Happy Birthday Baby"/"Apple Of My Eye"
626 "I Saw Mommy Kissing Santa Claus"/"Christmas Tears"

639 "Never On Sunday"/"Connie O" 1965
664 "Tonite Tonite"/"Since I Don't Have You"
713 "Little Boy"/"Silver Wings"
719 "My Mother's Eyes"/"Stay"

Phillips
40166 "Dawn"/"No Surfin' Today" 1964
40185 "Ronnie"/"Born To Wander"
40211 "Rag Doll"/"Silence Is Golden"
40225 "Save It For Me"/"Funny Face"
40238 "Big Man In Town"/"Little Angel"
40260 "Bye Bye Baby"/"Searching Wind" 1965
40278 "Toy Soldier"/"Betrayed"
40305 "Girl Come Running"/"Cry Myself To Sleep"
40317 "Let's Hang On"/"On Broadway Tonight"
40350 "Working My Way Back To You"/"Too Many Memories" 1966
40370 "Opus 17"/"Beggar's Parade"
40393 "I've Got You Under My Skin"/"Huggin' My Pillow"
40412 "Tell It To The Rain"/"Show Girl"
40433 "Beggin'"/"Dody" 1967
40460 "C'mon Marianne"/"Let's Ride Again"
40490 "Watch The Flowers Grow"/"Raven"
40523 "Will You Love Me Tomorrow"/"Around And Around" 1968
40542 "Saturday's Father"/"Goodbye Girl"
40577 "Electric Stories"/"Pity"
40597 "Idaho"/"Something's On Her Mind" 1969
40688 "Heartaches And Rain Drops"/"Lay Me Down"
40694 "Where Are My Dreams"/"Any Day Now"

As by the Wonder Who:

Vee Jay
717 "Peanuts"/"My Sugar" 1965
Phillips
40324 "Don't Think Twice"/"Sassy"

40380	"On The Good Ship Lollipop"/"You're Nobody Til Somebody Loves You"	1966
40471	"Lonesome Road"/"Around And Around"	1967

THE CRESTS

The Crests, a racially integrated New York City vocal group, first recorded two "do-wop" ballads on the small Joyce label. In particular, "Sweetest One" is now considered a rhythm and blues vocal group classic. The first national smash hit by The Crests was the romantic love ballad, "16 Candles," a best seller of 1958 and early 1959. "16 Candles" showcased the warm, strong vocals of lead singer Johnny Maestro.

Later hit records by The Crests included "Six Nights A Week," a song very similar to "16 Candles," and five uptempo singles: "The Angels Listened In," "A Year Ago Tonight," "Step By Step," "Trouble In Paradise" and "Isn't It Amazing." None of these follow-up successes approached the sales or notice of "16 Candles," The Crests' earliest and most durable hit. Later issues by The Crests, especially the Parkway label singles, were in somewhat of a soul music mold and had only modest sales. Maestro achieved popularity the second time around with The Brooklyn Bridge and had a fine ballad hit, "Worst That Could Happen." The Brooklyn Bridge was a new Johnny Maestro group with a professional pop sound.

Values

The two 45 RPM singles by The Crests on the Joyce label are now eagerly sought-after by vocal group collectors. "No One To Love Me" has sold for over $20, while "Sweetest One" can bring $15 to $20. "Pretty Little Girl" on Coed is a $10 to $12 single, while the far more popular "16 Candles" and later Coed label 45's generally bring $3.

Discography

As by The Crests:

Label / No.	Title	Year
Joyce		
103	"Sweetest One"/"My Juanita"	1957
105	"No One To Love Me"/"Wish She Was Mine"	
Coed		
501	"Pretty Little Girl"/"I Thank The Moon"	1958
506	"16 Candles"/"Beside You"	
509	"Six Nights A Week"/"I Do"	1959
511	"Flower Of Love"/"Molly Mae"	
515	"The Angels Listened In"/"I Thank The Moon"	
521	"A Year Ago Tonight"/"Paper Crown"	
525	"Step By Step"/"Gee"	1960
531	"Trouble In Paradise"/"Always You"	
535	"Journey Of Love"/"If My Heart Could Write A Letter"	
537	"Isn't It Amazing"/"Molly Mae"	
543	"In The Still Of The Night"/"Good Golly Miss Molly"	1961
561	"Little Miracles"/"Baby Gotta Know"	1962
Trans Atlas		
696	"The Actor"/"Three Tears In A Bucket"	1962
Selma		
311	"Guilty"/"Number One With Me"	1962
4000	"Did I Remember"/"Tears Will Fall"	
Cameo		
256	"I'll Be True"/"Over The Weekend"	1963

Coral
62403 "You Blew Out The Candles"/"A Love To Last A Lifetime" 1964

Times Square
6 "Baby"/"I Love You So" 1964

Scepter
12112 "I'm Stepping Out Of The Picture"/"Afraid To Love" 1965

Parkway
987 "Heartburn"/"Try Me" 1966
999 "I Care About You"/"Come See Me"
118 "My Time"/"Is It You"

As by The Brooklyn Bridge:

Buddah
60 "Little Red Boat By The River"/"From My Window" 1968
75 "Worst That Could Happen"/"Your Kite, My Kite"
95 "Welcome Me Love"/"Blessed Is The Rain" 1969
126 "Your Husband, My Wife"/"Upside Down"
139 "You'll Never Walk Alone"/"Minstrel Lady"

DANNY AND THE JUNIORS

Danny And The Juniors were responsible for two enormous hit records, "At The Hop" and the now classic follow-up rocker, "Rock And Roll Is Here To Stay"—possibly better known now in the nostalgic 70's than it was in the late 50's. By the early 60's, Danny And The Juniors were concentrating on the latest twist-spawned dance craze, with a loss of originality in material and spontaneity of approach.

Values

"At The Hop" on the original Singular label is in high demand on 45 RPM. This original version easily fetches $15 to $20, while the ABC reissue is worth about $3. Later ABC label releases are in the $3 to $5 area, while singles on Swan and later labels are worth about $2.

Discography

Label / No.	Title	Year
Singular		
711	"At The Hop"/"Sometimes"	1957
ABC		
9871	"At The Hop"/"Sometimes"	1957
9888	"Rock And Roll Is Here To Stay"/"School Boy Romance"	1958
9926	"In The Meantime"/"Dottie"	
9953	"A Thief"/"Crazy Cave"	1959
9978	"Feel So Lonely"/"Sassy Fran"	
10004	"Do You Love Me"/"Somehow I Can't Forget"	
10052	"Playing Hard To Get"/"Of Love"	
Swan		
4060	"Twistin' U.S.A."/"A Thousand Miles Away"	1960
4064	"O Holy Night"/"Candy Cane Sugary Cane"	
4068	"Pony Express"/"Daydreamer"	1961
4072	"Whisper Mister"/"Cha Cha Go Go"	
4082	"Back To The Hop"/"The Charleston Fish"	
4092	"Twistin' All Night Long" (With Freddie Cannon)/"Some Kind Of Nut"	1962
4100	"Doin' The Continental Walk"/"Do The Mashed Potatoes"	
4113	"Funny"/"We Got Soul"	

Guyden

2076	"Now And Then"/"Oh La La Limbo"	1963

Mercury

72240	"Let's Go Skiing"/"Sad Girl"	1964

DION AND THE BELMONTS

Dion And The Belmonts were first successful with the staccato-beat rock and roll release "I Wonder Why," one of the really excellent late 50's uptempo recordings. Dion And The Belmonts followed up with three downbeat ballads, "No One Knows," "Don't Pity Me" and "A Lover's Prayer," each featuring the engaging off-key lead vocal by Dion. The biggest hit Dion And The Belmonts had was the smoothly uptempo "A Teenager In Love" in 1959. In 1960, Dion and The Belmonts split up.

Dion as a single recorded a long string of rock and roll hits. Dion's first hit was "Lonely Teenager" in 1960, followed by "Runaround Sue" and "The Wanderer" in 1961, "Love Came To Me" in 1962, and two blues rockers borrowed from The Drifters, "Ruby Baby" and "Drip Drop" in 1963. In 1968, Dion made a short comeback, this time recording the gentle folk composition, "Abraham, Martin And John," a poetic contribution to the turbulent late 60's scene in America. The Belmonts experienced milder hit success with "Tell Me Why" and "Come On Little Angel," both skillfully rendered in intense rock and roll style.

Values

The 45 RPM single by Dion And The Timberlanes on the Mohawk label can fetch $8 to $10. The first single by Dion And The Belmonts, "I Wonder Why" on the original gray Laurie label can bring at least $5. Later Laurie label issues are in the $3 to $5 range. The earlier releases and singles with picture sleeves bring the higher prices. Singles by The Belmonts on Sabrina, and early Dion singles on both Laurie and Columbia, are worth $2 or $3.

Discography

As by Dion And The Timberlanes:

Mohawk

105	"The Chosen Few"/"Out In Colorado" (also on Jubilee 5294)	1957

As by Dion And The Belmonts:

Mohawk

106	"Teen Age Clementine"/"Santa Margerita"	
107	"We Went Away"/"Tag Along"	

Laurie

3013	"I Wonder Why"/"Teen Angel"	1958
3015	"No One Knows"/"(I Can't Go On) Rosalie"	
3021	"Don't Pity Me"/"Just You"	1959
3027	"A Teenager In Love"/"I've Cried Before"	
3035	"A Lover's Prayer"/"Every Little Thing I Do"	
3044	"Where Or When"/"That's My Desire"	
3052	"When You Wish Upon A Star"/"Wonderful Girl"	1960
3059	"In The Still Of The Night"/"A Funny Feeling"	

ABC

10868	"Bervumbav"/"My Girl The Month Of May"	
10896	"For Bobbie"/"Movin' Man"	1966

As by Dion:

Laurie

3070	"Lonely Teenager"/"Little Miss Blue"	1960
3081	"Havin' Fun"/"Northeast End Of The Corner"	1961
3090	"Kissin' Game"/"Heaven Help Me"	
3101	"Somebody Nobody Wants"/"Could Somebody Take My Place Tonight"	
3110	"Runaround Sue"/"Runaway Girl"	
3115	"The Wanderer"/"The Majestic"	
3123	"Lovers Who Wander"/"Born To Cry"	1962
3134	"Little Diane"/"Lost For Sure"	
3145	"Love Came To Me"/"Little Girl"	
3153	"Sandy"/"Faith"	1963
3171	"Come Go With Me"/"King Without A Queen"	
3187	"Lonely World"/"Tag Along"	
3225	"After The Dance"/"I'll Be Tired Of You"	1964
3240	"Shout"/"Little Girl"	

Columbia

42662	"Ruby Baby"/"He'll Only Hurt You"	1963
42776	"This Little Girl"/"The Loneliest Man In The World"	
42810	"Be Careful Of The Stones You Throw"/ "I Can't Believe"	
42852	"Donna The Prima Donna"/"You're Mine"	
42917	"Drip Drop"/"No One's Waiting For Me"	
42977	"The Road I'm On"/"I'm The Hoochie Koochie Man"	1964
43096	"Johnny B. Goode"/"Chicago Blues"	
43213	"Sweet Sweet Baby"/"Unloved Unwanted Me"	1965
43423	"Tomorrow Won't Bring The Rain"/"You Move Me Babe"	
43483	"Time In My Heart For You"/"Wake Up Baby"	
43692	"Two Ton Feather"/"So Much Younger"	1966

Laurie
3464 "Abraham Martin And John"/"Daddy Rolling Stone" 1968
3478 "Purple Haze"/"Dolphins" 1969
3495 "Both Sides Now"/"Sun Fun Song"

Warner Brothers
7401 "Sit Down Old Friend"/"Your Own Backyard"

As by The Belmonts:

Laurie
3080 "We Belong Together"/"Such A Long Way" 1961

Surprise
1000 "Tell Me Why"/"Smoke From Your Cigarette" (also on Sabrina 500)

Sabrina
500 "Tell Me Why"
501 "Don't Get Around Much Anymore"/"Searching For A New Love" 1962
502 "I Need Someone"/"The American Dance"
503 "I Confess"/"Hombre"
505 "Come On Little Angel"/"How About Me" 1963
507 "Farewell"/"Diddle-Dee-Dum"
509 "Acc-ent-Tehu-ate (The Positive)"/"Ann-Marie"
513 "Let's Call It A Day"/"Walk On By" 1964
517 "More Important Things To Do"/"Walk On By"
519 "C'mon Everybody"

United Artists
809 "Wintertime"/"I Don't Know Why"
904 "I Walked Away"
966 "I Got A Feeling"/"To Be With You" 1965
5007 "Come With Me"/"You're Like A Mystery"

THE TOKENS

The Tokens were a New York vocal group with a pleasant, finger-snapping pop sound. The group's first release, "While I Dream," featured The Tokens behind an early Neil Sedaka lead vocal. "Tonight I Fell In Love" on Warwick was an upbeat minor hit. "The Lion Sleeps Tonight" was a killer, one of the out-of-the-blue smash hits of all 1961. Precise falsetto harmony was the keynote of "The Lion Sleeps Tonight" and of other Tokens recordings, including the moody "He's In Town," a mid-60's hit. Their career was not limited to commercial recordings. The Tokens are also featured on numerous current TV advertising jingles, including the "Pan Am makes the going great" theme song.

Values

The solitary Melba label 45 is valued in the $5 range, while singles on Warwick and RCA can bring up to $3. All of the RCA singles have the accompanying picture sleeve, which can give these issues a slightly higher value.

Discography

As by The Tokens:

Melba

104	"While I Dream"/"I Love My Baby" (also on Oldies 45 105)	1957

Warwick

615	"Tonight I Fell In Love"/"I'll Always Love You"	1961

As by Johnny And The Tokens:

Warwick

658	"Taste Of A Tear"/"Never Till Now"	

As by The Tokens:

RCA

7896	"When I Go To Sleep At Night"/"Dry Your Eyes"	1961
7925	"Sincerely"/"When The Summer Is Through"	
7954	"The Lion Sleeps Tonight"/"Tina"	
7991	"B'wa Nina"/"Weeping River"	1962
8018	"The Riddle"/"Big Boat"	
8052	"La Bomba"/"A Token Of Love"	
8089	"I'll Do My Crying Tomorrow"/"Dream Angel Goodnight"	
8114	"A Bird Flies Out Of Sight"/"Wishing"	
8148	"Tonight I Met An Angel"/"Hindi Lullabye"	
8210	"Hear The Bells"/"A-B-C 1-2-3"	1963
8309	"Let's Go To The Drag Strip"/"2 Cars"	

Laurie

3180	"Please Write"/"I'll Always Love You"	1963

B.T. Puppy

500	"A Girl Named Arlene"/"Swing"	
502	"He's In Town"/"Oh Cathy"	1964
504	"You're My Girl"/"Havin' Fun"	
505	"Nobody But You"/"Mr. Cupid"	
507	"Sylvie Sleepin'"/"A Message To The World"	
512	"Only My Friend"/"Cattle Call"	1965
513	"The Bells Of St. Mary"/"Just One Smile"	
516	"The Three Bells"/"A Message To The World"	
518	"I Hear Trumpets Blow"/"Don't Cry, Sing Along With The Music"	1966

519 "Breezy"/"The Greatest Moments In A Girl's Life"
525 "Green Plant"/"Saloogy"
552 "Please Say You Want Me"/"Get A Job" 1967

As by The Four Winds:

B.T. Puppy
555 "Let It Ride"/"One Face In The Crowd" 1967

Swing
100 "Remember Last Summer"/"Strange Feelings"

As by The Buddies:

Swing
102 "On The Go"/"Only My Friend"

As by The Tokens:

Warner Brothers
5900 "Portrait Of My Love"/"She Comes And Goes" 1967
7056 "How Nice"/"It's A Happening World"
7099 "Ain't That Peculiar"/"Bye Bye Bye"
7169 "Till"/"Poor Man"
7183 "Mister Snail"/"Needles Of Evergreen"
7202 "Animal"/"Bathroom Wall"
7233 "The Banana Boat Song"/"Grandfather" 1968
7255 "The World Is Full Of Wonderful Things"/"Some People Sleep"
7280 "Go Away Little Girl—Young Girl"/"I Want To Make Love To You"
7323 "I Could Be"/"End Of The World"

Buddah
151 "She Lets Her Hair Down"/"Oh To Get Away" 1969
159 "Don't Worry Baby"/"Some People Sleep"

NEIL SEDAKA

Neil Sedaka began recording in a rhythm and blues vein with The Tokens vocal group on the Melba label. However, none of Sedaka's earliest material generated hit power until he recorded "The Diary" in 1958. "The Diary," a ballad with a very strong rhythm and blues flavor, possessed a striking similarity to "Tears On My Pillow" by Little Anthony And The Imperials (End 1027). In fact, Little Anthony And The Imperials recorded a simultaneous version of "The Diary" (End 1038), however the Sedaka single was the definitive hit. Neil Sedaka followed with three pop-flavored rockers, "I Go Ape," "Oh, Carol," written about Carole King, and the uncharacteristically country and western sounding "Run Sampson Run."

Into the early 60's, Neil Sedaka scored with such lively upbeat singles as "Calendar Girl" in 1960, "Happy Birthday Sweet Sixteen" in 1961, the cha-cha of "Breaking Up Is Hard To Do" in 1962 and "Alice In Wonderland" in 1963—all major top ten hits. Neil Sedaka was one of the first rock and roll artists to use multiple tracking of his vocal performance to create the illusion of a back-up vocal group. This tracking, which he used frequently, enhanced the good-natured sound of his hit records. Sedaka returned in 1974-75 with "Laughter In The Rain."

Values

Neil Sedaka's 45 RPM singles on Decca, Guyden and Pyramid can bring from $3 to $5. Many of the RCA singles (up to RCA 8007) fetch over $2, especially with picture sleeves.

Discography

Decca

30520	"Laura Lee"/"Snowtime"	1957

RCA

7408	"The Diary"/"No Vacancy"	1958
7473	"I Go Ape"/"Moon Of Gold"	1959
7530	"You Gotta Learn Your Rhythm And Blues"/"Crying My Heart Out For You"	
7595	"Oh, Carol"/"One Way Ticket"	
7709	"Stairway To Heaven"/"Forty Winks Away"	1960
7781	"Run Sampson Run"/"You Mean Everything To Me"	
7829	"Calendar Girl"/"The Same Old Fool"	
7874	"Little Devil"/"I Must Be Dreaming"	1961
7922	"Sweet Little You"/"I Found My World In You"	
7957	"Happy Birthday Sweet Sixteen"/"Don't Lead Me On"	
8007	"King Of Clowns"/"Walk With Me"	1962
8046	"Breaking Up Is Hard To Do"/"As Long As I Live"	
8086	"Next Door To An Angel"/"I Belong To You"	
8137	"Alice In Wonderland"/"Circulate"	1963
8169	"Let's Go Steady Again"/"Waiting For Never"	
8209	"The Dreamer"/"Look Inside Your Heart"	
8254	"Bad Girl"/"Wait Til You See My Baby"	
8341	"Without A Song"/"The Closest Thing To Heaven"	1964
8382	"Sunny"/"She'll Never Be You"	
8453	"Too Late"/"I Hope He Breaks Your Heart"	
8511	"Let The People Talk"/"In The Chapel With You"	
8637	"The World Through A Tear"/"High On A Mountain"	1965
8737	"The Answer To A Prayer"/"Blue Boy"	1966
9004	"Too Late"/"We Can Make It If We Try"	

Guyden

2004	"Fly Don't Fly On Me"/"Ring A Rockin'" (also on Legion 133)	1961

Pyramid
623 "Oh Delilah"/"Neil's Twist" 1962

SGC
005 "Had A Good Thing Going"/"Star Crossed Lovers"
008 "Rainy Jane"

THE PLAYMATES

The Playmates were essentially a pop-ballad vocal group in the mold of the earlier Crew Cuts. "Jo-Ann," their earliest hit, was a successful romantic teenage ballad. "Darling It's Wonderful," The Playmates' only cover record was borrowed from The Lovers (Lamp 2005) rhythm and blues vocal group. However, The Playmates' major hit was the novelty "Beep Beep," a tedious description of a speeding duel between a Cadillac and a Rambler. Three hit follow-ups were similarly innocuous, the overly cute "What Is Love" along with two adolescent love songs, "Wait For Me" and "Little Miss Stuck Up."

Values

The Playmates' 45 RPM Roulette label singles are rarely worth more than $2.

Discography

Apex
76189 "Island Girl"/"Darling It's Wonderful" 1957

Roulette
4003 "Barefoot Girl"/"Pretty Woman" 1957
4022 "Darling It's Wonderful"/"Magic Shoes"
4037 "Jo-Ann"/"You Can't Stop Me From Dreaming" 1958

4056 "Let's Be Lovers"/"Give Me Another Chance"
4072 "Don't Go Home"/"Can't You Get It Through Your Head"
4100 "While The Record Goes Around"/"The Day I Died"
4115 "Beep Beep"/"Your Love"
4136 "Star Love"/"The Ting-A-Ma-Jig" 1959
4160 "What Is Love"/"I Am"
4200 "First Love"/"A Ciu-E"
4211 "The Song Everybody's Singing"/"On The Beach"
4227 "These Things I Offer You"/"Second Chance" 1960
4252 "Parade Of Pretty Girls"/"Our Wedding Day"
4276 "Wait For Me"/"Eyes Of An Angel"
4322 "Little Miss Stuck Up"/"Real Life" 1961
4370 "Tell Me What She Said"/"Cowboys Never Cry"
4393 "Wimoweh"/"One Little Kiss"
4417 "A Rose And A Star"/"Bachelor Flat" 1962
4432 "Keep Your Hands In Your Pockets"/"The Cop On The Beat"
4464 "What A Funny Way To Show It"/"Petticoats Fly"

THE ROYAL TEENS

The Royal Teens' first, biggest and most memorable hit was the stroll beat "Short Shorts." "Short Shorts" was an unbeatable combination, catchy, timely lyrics with basic rock and roll vocals and instrumentation. As of this writing, the "Short Shorts" instrumental track has been transferred to a similar record dealing with the naked art of streaking. Topical lyrics were the common denominator to other Royal Teens' hits such as "Big Name Button" and "Leotards." Their recordings on the Capitol label included the appealing rocker, "Believe Me" with the novelty flip "Little Cricket," a major hit.

Values

Singles by The Royal Teens on 45 RPM are in great demand. "Short Shorts" on the obscure Power label can bring over $5, as do "Leotards" and "Little Trixie." The ABC label releases bring from $2 to $3. The Capitol label singles "Believe Me" and "With You" are valued at $5, while "The Moon's Not Meant For Lovers" is a sought-after record, worth as much as $10.

Discography

Power

215	"Short Shorts"/"Planet Rock"	1958

ABC

9882	"Short Shorts"/"Planet Rock"	1958
9918	"Big Name Button"/"Sham Rock"	
9945	"Harvey's Got A Girl Friend"/"Hangin' Around"	
9955	"My Kind Of Dream"/"Open The Door"	

Mighty

111	"Royal Blue"/"Leotards"	
200	"Little Trixie"/"My Memories Of You"	

Power

113	"Mad Gas"/"Sittin' With My Baby" (also on Astra 1012)	

Capitol

4261	"Believe Me"/"Little Cricket"	1959
4335	"The Moon's Not Meant For Lovers"/ "Was It A Dream"	

4402 "With You"/"It's The Talk Of The Town"

Jubilee
5418 "Short Short Twist"/"Royal Twist" 1962
(instrumental—also on All New 1415)

Swan
4200 "I'll Love You Part 1 & Part 2"

THE TEDDY BEARS

The Teddy Bears were a short-lived trio, the vehicle for the first Phil Spector production in his legendary "To Know Him Is To Love Him," a smash hit of 1958. "To Know Him Is To Love Him" possessed a hypnotic chanting sound, a totally different type of rock and roll for the late 50's. Though follow-up releases such as "Wonderful Loveable You" were as warm and professionally produced as "To Know Him Is To Love Him," none achieved the instant hit appeal of this milestone recording. Phil Spector's next landmark success was not until 1961 and his again short-lived Philles label.

Values

Single releases by The Teddy Bears on both Dore and Imperial are generally worth $3 to $5, at most. The higher price applies to the obscure discs, especially "Seven Lonely Days," the last recording.

Discography

Dore
503 "To Know Him Is To Love Him"/"Don't You Worry My Little Pet" 1958
520 "Wonderful Loveable You"/"Til You'll Be Mine" 1959

Imperial
5562 "Oh Why"/"I Don't Need You Anymore" 1959
5581 "If You Only Knew"/"You Said Goodbye"
5594 "Seven Lonely Days"/"Don't Go Away"

THE FLEETWOODS

The Fleetwoods, a trio from the Pacific Northwest, performed downbeat arrangements in a polished and diffident ballad style. "Come Softly To Me" showcased the gentle harmony of the trio, which used a male lead with soft female accompaniment. "Come Softly To Me" was a best seller of 1959. "Mr. Blue," released later in 1959, was even more successful—apparently it struck a sympathetic chord with its self-indulgent theme of melancholy. Follow-up best sellers were often drawn from early rhythm and blues material, such as The Orioles' "Runaround" (Jubilee 5172) and "Confidential," a song original to Sonny Knight (Vita 137). "The Great Imposter," a Fleetwoods' original, was their last major hit.

Values

The Fleetwoods' first two Dolton label singles, especially "Come Softly To Me" on the Dolphin label —before the label's name change to Dolton—can bring around $3, while later issues are worth $2 or less.

Discography

Dolphin
1 "Come Softly To Me"/"I Care So Much" 1959
(also on Liberty 55188)

Dolton
3 "Graduation's Here"/"Oh Lord Let It Be"

5	"Mr. Blue"/"You Mean Everything To Me"	
15	"Outside My Window"/"Magic Star"	1960
22	"Runaround"/"Truly Do"	
27	"Last One To Know"/"Dormilona"	
30	"Confidential"/"I Love You So"	1961
40	"Tragedy"/"Little Miss Sad One"	
45	"(He's) The Great Imposter"/"Poor Little Girl"	1962
49	"Billy Old Buddy"/"Trouble"	
62	"Lovers By Night—Strangers By Day"/ "They Tell Me It's Summer"	
74	"You Should Have Been There"/"Sure Is Lonesome Downtown"	1963
75	"Goodnight My Love"/"Jimmy Beware"	
86	"Baby Bye-O"/"What'll I Do"	
93	"Lonesome Town"/"Ruby Red Baby Blue"	
97	"Ska Light Ska Bright"/"Ten Times Blue"	1964
98	"Mr. Sandman"/"This Is My Prayer"	
310	"Rainbow"/"Just As I Need You"	
315	"For Lovin' Me"	

THE MYSTICS

The Mystics, still another New York City vocal group, recorded for the Laurie label, and thus were somewhat overshadowed by the very popular Dion And The Belmonts, who were also on the Laurie label and had a similar style. The Mystics recorded almost fragile rock and roll, evident in the fast tempo "Hushabye." "Hushabye" was a national smash hit, the only one for the short career of The Mystics.

Values

The Mystics' singles are generally in the $2 to $3

range. "Hushabye," a best seller, can go for less than $2; the more obscure "White Cliffs Of Dover" may fetch $3.

Discography

Laurie

3028	"Hushabye"/"Adam And Eve"	1959
3038	"So Tenderly"/"Don't Take The Stars"	
3047	"All Through The Night"/"I Begin (To Think Of You Again)"	1960
3058	"White Cliffs Of Dover"/"Blue Star"	
3086	"Star Crossed Lovers"/"Goodbye Mr. Blues"	1961
3104	"A Sunday Kind Of Love"/"Darling I Know"	

THE ECHOES

Another vocal group with a decidedly gentle rock and roll sound, The Echoes recorded one hit, the medium tempo "Baby Blue." The Echoes were quickly submerged after issuing just a few early 60's singles.

Values

Singles by The Echoes are worth $2 or $3, while the hit "Baby Blue" fetches less than $2.

Discography

Seg-Way

103	"Baby Blue"/"Boomerang"	1961

106 "Sad Eyes"/"It's Rainin' "
1002 "Gee Oh Gee"/"Angel Of My Heart"

JAY AND THE AMERICANS

Jay And The Americans had a distinctive pop-styled approach to their music; few of the rhythm and blues influences noted with most other New York groups are found in their recordings. "Tonight," Jay And The Americans' initial release, was taken from the score of *West Side Story* and as a single was fairly successful. "She Cried," their next release, was an appealing ballad and gave the group their first national hit. Other major hits by Jay And The Americans were the upbeat "Come A Little Bit Closer" in 1965 and "Cara Mia" in 1966, both rendered in a unique Latin-based tempo. "This Magic Moment," a 1969 release, achieved moderately successful sales.

Values

Single releases by Jay And The Americans on the early United Artists label (up to United Artists 693) can bring about $2, especially with a picture sleeve.

Discography

United Artists

415	"Tonight"/"The Other Girls"	1961
479	"She Cried"/"Dawning"	
504	"Tomorrow"/"Yes"	1962
556	"Strangers Tomorrow"/"What's The Use"	
626	"Only In America"/"My Clair DeLune"	1963
669	"Come Dance With Me"/"Look In My Eyes World"	
693	"To Wait For Love"/"Friday"	

759 "Come A Little Bit Closer"/"Goodbye Boys Goodbye" 1964
805 "Let's Lock The Door"/"I'll Remember You"
845 "Think Of The Good Times"/"If You Were Mine Girl"
881 "Cara Mia"/"When It's All Over" 1965
919 "Some Enchanted Evening"/"Girl"
948 "Sunday And Me"/"Through This Doorway"
992 "Why Can't You Bring Me Home"/ "Baby Stop Your Crying"
50016 "Crying"/"I Don't Need A Friend" 1966
50046 "Living Above Your Head"/"Look At Me—What Do You See"
50094 "Raining In My Sunshine"/"The Reason For Living" 1967
50139 "You Ain't As Hip As All That Baby"/ "Nature Boy"
50196 "Yellow Forest"/"Got Hung Up Along The Way"
50222 "French Provincial"/"Shanghai Noodle Factory" 1968
50282 "No Other Love"/"No, I Don't Know Her"
50448 "You Ain't Gonna Wake Up Crying"/ "Gemini"
50475 "This Magic Moment"/"Since I Don't Have You" 1969
50510 "When You Dance"/"No, I Don't Know Her"
50535 "Hushabye"/"Gypsy Woman"
50567 "Learnin' How To Fly"/"I'd Kill For The Love Of A Lady"

THE REGENTS

The Regents had one quick Gee label smash hit with the aggressive "Barbara Ann," an excellent straightforward rock and roll record. Later recordings were also fine performances but, with the exception of "Runaround," did not have the solid rock and roll feel of the exciting "Barbara Ann."

Values

"Barbara Ann" and "Runaround" by The Regents were both hits but at most fetch $2. The other two single releases, especially the poorer selling "Liar," are now worth up to $3.

Discography

Cousins

1002	"Barbara Ann"/"I'm So Lonely" (also on Gee 1065)	1961

Gee

1071	"Runaround"/"Laura My Darling"	
1073	"Liar"/"Don't Be A Fool"	
1075	"Lonesome Boy"/"Oh Baby"	1962

Philadelphia Rock and Roll

The alleged payola scandal of the very late 50's was frequently used as a guise by those who wanted to help with the destruction of rock and roll. Anti-rock and roll protests and satire were staples of the late 50's media. Disc jockeys throughout the country smashed rock and roll recordings on the air—78's were the easiest discs to shatter dramatically—and record-burning campaigns were not infrequent. Admittedly, very little important was happening in the rock and roll of 1959 and 1960, still the death knell of rock and roll was sounded presumptively.

Philadelphia Rock And Roll proved that rock and roll was indeed not dead, though some critics felt that the sound was shallow and amounted to the dying gasp of rock and roll. Regardless, this Philadelphia sound was enormously popular, amounting to the last important pop rock and roll sound of the 50's.

The United States had temporarily lost Elvis Presley, the king of rock and roll, to the draft in 1958. The void was partially filled by the likes of Frankie Avalon, Fabian and Bobby Rydell, whose best work was found in their earliest releases. By the early 60's, singles by these artists revealed few traces of this early rock and roll sound.

FRANKIE AVALON

The first recorded performance by Frankie Avalon was the solo instrumental "Trumpet Sorrento," with the label credit reading "by 11 year old Frankie Avalon."

It was not until his later teen years that Avalon recorded his first two major hits, the bop-tempo "De De Dinah" and "Gingerbread." These squeaky voiced performances were very danceable hits by Avalon, the original exponent of the late 50's Philadelphia Rock And Roll sound, which was heavily promoted by a nationally broadcast TV rock and roll dance program. Avalon's biggest hit was the sparkling pop-classic "Venus."

Though Frankie Avalon persisted with single releases well into the early 60's, he had no major hits after 1959. Both "Bobby Sox To Stockings" and "Why" were polished yet undistinguished ballads, released in a futile attempt to recapture the magic of "Venus." "Just Ask Your Heart" was Frankie Avalon's last solid rock and roll release, an energetic vocal with strong rhythmic backing. "Just Ask Your Heart" was dramatic proof of Avalon's more mature vocal ability, with no hint of the distinctive, high-pitched nasal sound in "De De Dinah." During two short years of recording success, Frankie Avalon swiftly rose, then declined as the premier rock and roll superstar.

Values

Long before the beginning of his rock and roll career, Frankie Avalon recorded and had issued a trumpet solo on the X label subsidiary of RCA, "Trumpet Sorrento." This 45 RPM release was far from popular; today it is in demand by collectors of Frankie Avalon and fetches $10. The earliest 45 RPM singles by Avalon on Chancellor (to Chancellor 1011) are fairly scarce and bring from $3 to $5, while later issues (to Chancellor 1026) are generally worth about $2.

Discography

X

0006	"Trumpet Sorrento"/"The Book"	ca. 1952
0026	"Trumpet Tarantella"/"Dormi, Dormi"	

Chancellor

1004	"Jiving With The Saints"/"Cupid" (by Rocco And The Saints)	1957
1006	"Teacher's Pet"/"Shy Guy"	
1011	"De De Dinah"/"Ooh La La"	1958
1016	"You Excite Me"/"Darlin'"	
1021	"Gingerbread"/"Blue Betty"	
1026	"I'll Wait For You"/"What Little Girl"	
1031	"Venus"/"I'm Broke" (re-issued on Chancellor 1114)	1959
1036	"Bobby Sox To Stockings"/"A Boy Without A Girl"	
1040	"Just Ask Your Heart"/"Two Fools"	
1045	"Why"/"Swingin' On A Rainbow"	
1048	"Don't Throw Away All Those Teardrops"/"Talk, Talk, Talk"	1960
1052	"Where Are You"/"Tuxedo Junction"	
1056	"Togetherness"/"Don't Let Love Pass Me By"	
1065	"Puppet Song"/"A Perfect Love"	
1071	"All Of Everything"/"Call Me Anytime"	1961
1077	"Gotta Get A Girl"/"Who Else But You"	

1081 "Voyage To The Bottom Of The Sea"/ "The Summer Of '61"
1087 "True True Love"/"Married" 1962
1095 "Sleeping Beauty"/"The Lonely Bit"
1101 "After You've Gone"/"If You Don't Think I'm Leaving"
1107 "You Are Mine"/"Italiano"
1115 "A Miracle"/"Don't Let Me Stand In Your Way" 1963
1125 "Welcome Home"/"Dance Bossa Nova"
1131 "My Ex-Best Friend"/"First Love Never Dies" 1964
1134 "Come Fly With Me"
1135 "Cleopatra"/"Heartbeats"
1139 "Beach Party"/"Don't Stop Now"

FABIAN

Fabian Forte projected an element of virility into the otherwise very controlled and restrained pop-flavored Philadelphia rock and roll sound. The material selected for this sixteen-year-old instant teenage idol was meant to capitalize on a theme of sexual prowess, rendered with a touch of adolescent defiance. "I'm A Man," the snarling "Turn Me Loose," and the similarly boisterous "Tiger" and "Hound Dog Man" created for Fabian the same type of image —self-proclaimed manliness—professed by Bo Diddley and other blues artists of the mid-50's.

Perhaps not coincidentally, Bo Diddley's initial single release was also entitled "I'm A Man" (Checker 814), although it was a different composition. None of Fabian's recordings after 1959 became major hits—a failing shared by his Chancellor label counterpart, Frankie Avalon. Despite his limited vocal talents, Fabian managed to add a new dimension to the Philadelphia pop sound with his direct, on-target rock and roll.

Values

Fabian's first two recordings on Chancellor can bring $5, while later issues, beginning with his first hit "Turn Me Loose" rarely fetch over $2.

Discography

With The Four Dates

Chancellor

1020	"I'm In Love"/"Shivers"	1958
1024	"Be My Steady Date"/"Lilly Lou"	

As by Fabian:

Chancellor

1029	"I'm A Man"/"Hypnotized"	1959
1033	"Turn Me Loose"/"Stop Thief"	
1037	"Tiger"/"Mighty Cold"	
1041	"Got The Feeling"/"Come On And Get Me"	
1044	"Hound Dog Man"/"This Friendly World"	
1047	"String Along"/"About This Thing Called Love"	1960
1051	"I'm Gonna Sit Right Down And Write Myself A Letter"/"Strollin' In The Springtime"	
1055	"King Of Love"/"Tomorrow"	
1061	"Kissin' And Twistin'"/"Long Before"	
1067	"You Know You Belong To Somebody Else"/"Hold On"	1961
1072	"Grapevine"/"David & Goliath"	
1079	"The Love That I'm Giving You"/"You're Only Young Once"	
1084	"Dream Factory"/"Girl Like You"	
1086	"Kansas City"/"Tongue Tied"	
1092	"Wild Party"/"Gospel Truth"	

Dot

16413	"She's Stayin' Inside With Me"/"Break Down And Cry"	1962

DICKEY DOO AND THE DON'TS

Dickey Doo And The Don'ts were basically an instrumental rock and roll group. "Click Clack" was a pleasant, pop-sounding rock beat hit. In contrast, "Nee Nee Na Na Nu Nu" was a strong rocking instrumental, not only their best record but still an off-beat 50's rock and roll classic. Later recordings by Dickey Doo And The Don'ts tended towards a bland sound, occasionally even corny as is evident with the sing-along sound of "Wabash Cannonball."

Values

Singles by Dickey Doo And The Don'ts are worth $2 or $3. The scarcest and most sought-after is the group's best rock and roll single "Nee Nee Na Na Nu Nu," often valued up to $5.

Discography

Swan

4001	"Click Clack"/"Did You Cry"	1958
4006	"Nee Nee Na Na Nu Nu"/"Flip Top Box"	
4014	"Wild Party"/"Leave Me Alone"	
4025	"Teardrops Will Fall"/"Come With Us"	1959
4033	"Dear Heart Don't Cry"/"Ballad Of A Train"	
4046	"Wabash Cannonball"/"The Drums Of Richard A Doo"	

BILLIE AND LILLIE

In a decade of such basic rhythm and blues duets as Shirley And Lee or Gene And Eunice, Billie And Lillie possessed a contrastingly relaxed and typically pop Philadelphia sound. Hits by Billie And Lillie included two very pleasant, cha-cha (renamed "chalypso" in 1958) beat novelties: "La Dee Dah," with lyrics which incorporated the titles of just about every current popular hit, and "Lucky Lady Bug."

Values

Recordings by Billie And Lillie on the Swan label generally bring from $2 to $3. The ABC label issues have a fine "do-wop" vocal group sound and are worth some $5.

Discography

Swan

4002	"La Dee Dah"/"The Monster"	1958
4005	"Happiness"/"Creepin' Crawlin' Cryin'"	
4011	"Hangin' On To You"/"The Greasy Spoon"	
4020	"Lucky Lady Bug"/"I Promise You"	
4030	"Aloysius Horatio Thomas The Cat"/ "Tumbled Down"	1959
4036	"Bells Bells Bells"/"Honeymoonin'"	
4051	"The Ins And Outs"/"Free For All"	1960
4058	"Over The Mountain Across The Sea"/ "That's The Way The Cookie Crumbles"	
4069	"Banana's"/"Ain't Comin' Back"	1961

ABC

10421	"Love Me Sincerely"/"Whip It To Me Baby"	1963

10489 "Why I Love Billy"/"Carry Me Across The Threshold"

Cameo

412 "Nothing Moves"/"Two Of Us" 1964

BOBBY RYDELL

Bobby Rydell brought the ebbing Philadelphia school of rock and roll into the early 60's with two engaging rock and roll hits, "We Got Love" and "Wild One." Rydell's hit string was with strictly upbeat material such as "Swingin' School" and the successful restyling of "Volare" in 1960, and in 1961 with "Good Time Baby" and "The Fish," a dance record happily lost among the wide assortment of soundalike twist imitations. Cameo/Parkway label's major talent was Chubby Checker, with whom Bobby Rydell was teamed for two mediocre singles, "Jingle Bell Rock" and "Teach Me How To Twist." The year 1963 was when both the Philadelphia Sound and twist fervor expired, however Rydell did manage to have some minor hits during that particular year.

Values

Singles by Bobby Rydell on both the Veko and Venise labels can command over $5. Rydell's initial Cameo label release, "Please Don't Be Mad," was sung with a fine rhythm and blues vocal group and brings up to $10. Later releases by Rydell (after Cameo 167) were hits and are generally worth $2 or $3.

Discography

Venise

201 "Fatty Fatty"/"Happy Happy" 1958

Veko

731 "Fatty Fatty"/"Dream Age"

Cameo

160 "Please Don't Be Mad"/"Makin' Time" 1958
164 "All I Want Is You"/"For You, For You" 1959
167 "Kissin' Time"/"You'll Never Tame Me"
169 "We Got Love"/"I Dig Girls" (also on Time 1006)
171 "Wild One"/"Little Bitty Girl" 1960
175 "Swingin' School"/"Ding A Ling"
179 "Volare"/"I'll Do It Again"
182 "Sway"/"Groovy Tonight"
186 "Good Time Baby"/"Cherie" 1961
190 "That Old Black Magic"/"Don't Be Afraid"
192 "The Fish"/"The Third House"
201 "I Wanna Thank You"/"The Door To Paradise"
205 "Jingle Bell Rock"/"Jingle Bell Rock Imitations" (with Chubby Checker)
209 "I've Got Bonnie"/"Lose Her" 1962
214 "Teach Me To Twist"/"Swingin' Together" (with Chubby Checker)
217 "I'll Never Dance Again"/"Gee It's Wonderful"
228 "The Cha Cha Cha"/"The Best Man Cried"
242 "Butterfly Baby"/"Love Is Blind" 1963
252 "Wildwood Days"/"Will You Be My Baby"
265 "Little Queenie"/"The Woodpecker Song"
272 "Childhood Sweetheart"/"Let's Make Love Tonight"
280 "Forget Him"/"Love Love Go Away"
309 "Make Me Forget"/"Little Girl You've Had A Busy Day" 1964
320 "A World Without Love"/"Our Faded Love"
361 "Ciao Ciao Bambino"/"Voce De La Notte"

1070	"A Message From Bobby"/"Forget Him"	
Capitol		
5305	"I Just Can't Say Goodbye"/"Two Is The Loneliest Number"	1964
5352	"Diana"/"Stranger In The World"	1965
5438	"Side Show"/"The Joker"	
5513	"It Takes Two"/"When I See That Girl Of Mine"	
5556	"The Word For Today"/"Roses In The Snow"	1966
5696	"She Was The Girl"/"Not You"	

FREDDIE CANNON

Freddie "Boom Boom" Cannon was in the forefront of the early 60's Philadelphia rock and roll school. Cannon was probably the most talented of all the major Philadelphia male vocal stars, and he picked up where Frankie Avalon and Fabian left off. However, unlike Frankie Avalon's teenage sweetness or Fabian's patented surliness, Freddie Cannon specialized in rousing energy. This energy was apparent in such exciting hits as "Tallahassee Lassie," "Okefenokee" and the rock and roll restyling of "Way Down Yonder In New Orleans." Each of these records had the kind of vitality that made them fun to listen to. After all, rock and roll is at its best when it's fun, and Freddie Cannon gave his recordings this quality.

All of his releases were whirlwind rock and roll and most were hits, either major or minor. Among Freddie Cannon's stronger recordings were "Jump Over," the unusual, guitar-paced "Buzz Buzz A Diddle It," the bouncy Palisades Park" and two very clever arrangements, "Abigail Beecher (Our History Teacher)" and "OK Wheeler, The Used Car Dealer." The first two or three years of the 60's were vacant of good rock and roll. Freddie Cannon was one of very few performers who maintained a constant flow of good time rock and roll recordings during this period.

Values

Singles by Freddie Cannon on both Swan and Warner Brothers were hits and sold well; thus, even though they are in demand, they rarely are worth more than $2 or $3.

Discography

Swan

4031	"Tallahassie Lassie"/"You Know"	1959
4038	"Okefenokee"/"Kookie Hat"	
4043	"Way Down Yonder In New Orleans"/ "Fractured"	
4050	"Chattanooga Shoe Shine Boy"/"Boston"	1960
4053	"Jump Over"/"The Urge"	
4057	"Happy Shades Of Blue"/"Cuernavaca Choo Choo"	
4061	"Humdinger"/"My Blue Heaven"	
4066	"2088"/"The Muskrat Ramble"	1961
4071	"Buzz Buzz A Diddle It"/"Opportunity"	
4078	"Transistor Sister"/"Walk To The Moon"	
4083	"For Me And My Gal"/"Blue Plate Special"	
4096	"Teen Queen Of The Week"/"Wild Guy"	1962
4106	"Palisades Park"/"June July And August"	
4117	"What's Gonna Happen When Summer's Gone"/"Broadway"	
4122	"If You Were A Rock And Roll Record"/ "The Truth, Ruth"	
4132	"Four Letter Man"/"Come On And Love Me"	
4139	"Patty Baby"/"Betty Jean"	1963
4149	"Everybody Monkey"/"Oh Gloria"	

4155	"Do What The Hippies Do"/"That's The Way Girls Are"	

Warner Brothers

5409	"Abigail Beecher"/"All American Girl"	1964
5434	"OK Wheeler, The Used Car Dealer"/ "Odie Cologne"	
5448	"Gotta Good Thing Goin'"/"Summertime USA"	
5487	"Little Autograph Seeker"/"Too Much Monkey Business"	
5615	"In The Night"/"Little Miss A Go Go Go"	
5648	"Action"/"Beachwood City"	1965
5666	"Let Me Show You Where It's At"/"The Old Rag Man"	
5673	"She's Something Else"	
5693	"The Dedication Song"/"Come On Come On"	1966
5810	"Hokie Pokie Girl"/"Greatest Show On Earth"	
5832	"Natalie"/"The Laughing Song"	
5859	"Run For The Sun"/"Use Your Imagination"	
5876	"A Happy Clown"/"In My Wildest Dream"	
7019	"Mavericks Flat"/"To The Poet"	
7075	"Cincinnati Woman"	

We Make Rock N Roll Records

1601	"Rock Around The Clock"/"Sock It To The Judge"	1968
1604	"Sea Cruise"/"She's A Friday Night Fox"	

Royal-American

288	"Blossom Dear"/"Strawberry Wine"	

THE DOVELLS

Still another New Jersey-Philadelphia vocal group, The Dovells were among the most successful of early Parkway label artists. "The Bristol Stomp" was a solid, uptempo dance step. Released during the early 60's period of dance crazes, "The Bristol Stomp" developed into a major national hit. Parkway/Cameo had an apparent knack for creating rock and roll dance hits, as The Dovells were successful with such follow-ups as the "Mope-itty Mope Stomp," complete with a strange hard-hitting beat and deadpan nonsense lyrics; the rocking "Bristol Twistin' Annie," the slower "Hully Gully Baby" and "You Can't Sit Down." With their friendly, engaging vocal style, The Dovells transformed upbeat material into top ten hits.

Values

The first two releases by The Dovells, "No No No" and "Out In The Cold Again," the original flip to "The Bristol Stomp," were limited pressings and thus can bring over $3. The hit pressing of "The Bristol Stomp" and the next five or six single releases, especially with a picture sleeve, are worth $2.

Discography

Parkway

819	"No No No"/"Letters Of Love"	1961
827	"The Bristol Stomp"/"Out In The Cold Again"	
827	"The Bristol Stomp"/"Letters Of Love"	
833	"Mope-itty Mope Stomp"/"Doing The New Continental"	
838	"Bristol Twistin' Annie"/"The Actor"	1962
845	"Hully Gully Baby"/"Your Last Chance"	
855	"The Jitterbug"/"Kissin' In The Kitchen"	
861	"Save Me Baby"/"You Can't Run Away From Yourself"	
867	"You Can't Sit Down"/"Stompin' Everywhere"	1963

867 "You Can't Sit Down"/"Wildwood Days"
882 "Betty In Bermudas"/"Dance The Froog"
889 "No No No"/"Stop Monkeyin' Around"
901 "Be My Girl"/"Dragster On The Prowl" 1964
911 "One Potato"/"Happy Birthday Just The Same"
925 "What In The World's Come Over You"/"Watusi With Lucy"

Swan
4231 "Happy"/"Alright" 1964

West Coast Rock and Roll

◉

In the very late 50's and early 60's, several important West Coast artists emerged with best selling singles. The styles of each were considerably different—from the coy rock and roll of Annette, the steady surf rock of Jan And Dean and The Beach Boys, to the pioneer hard rock of the Pacific Northwest's Kingsmen, Wailers and Paul Revere And The Raiders.

JAN AND ARNIE/JAN AND DEAN/ THE NORTONES

As Jan And Arnie, the duet was fairly successful with three rhythmic rock beat releases, "Jennie Lee" was by far the best seller of the lot. As Jan (Berry) And Dean (Torrence), the pair continued recording with an arresting rock beat and deadpan vocal work. "Baby Talk" was a good selling 1959 hit. However, it was not until the surf rock craze of 1963 that Jan And Dean scored with the national smash hit, "Surf City," a song very similar to the early hits of The Beach Boys. Follow-up singles included such novelty surf material as "Honolulu Lulu," and hot rod compositions like "Drag City," "The Little Old Lady From Pasadena" and the strangely prophetic "Dead Man's Curve." Jan Berry was later involved in a near fatal car wreck under circumstances strangely similar to the lyrics of "Dead Man's Curve" and survived only after being in a long coma. Mid-60's recordings by Jan And Dean were the faddish "Sidewalk Surfin'," the sadly bitter "The Universal Coward," a repudiation of protests to the war in Viet Nam, and the very topical "Batman." In the wake of tragedy to Jan Berry, the duet stopped recording in the late 60's. In the very early 70's, they returned to record as The Legendary Masked Surfers. During the 60's, Jan And Dean can be credited with an impressive string of frivolous, timely and very popular rock and roll releases.

Values

The Jan And Arnie singles on the Arwin label are excellent simple rock and roll, prime wants for all collectors of Jan And Dean and surf rock. "Jennie Lee" can bring $3, the other two about $5. The two singles by The Nortones on Warner Brothers bring $3 to $5. Dore and Challenge label singles by Jan And Dean are worth over $2, while the consistently popular Liberty singles bring less than $2. With picture sleeves the Liberty issues are a firm $2.

Discography

As by Jan And Arnie:

Arwin

108 "Jennie Lee"/"Gotta Get A Date" 1958

111 "Gas Money"/"Bonnie Lou" (also on Dot 16116)
113 "I Love Linda"/"The Beat That Can't Be Beat"

As by The Nortones:

Warner Brothers
5065 "Susie Jones" 1959
5115 "Boy"/"Smile Just Smile"

As by Jan And Dean:

Dore
522 "Baby Talk"/"Jeanette Get Your Hair Done" 1959
531 "There's A Girl"/"My Heart Sings"
539 "Clementine"/"You're On My Mind" 1960
548 "White Tennis Sneakers"/"Cindy"
555 "We Go Together"/"Rosie Lane"
576 "Gee"/"Such A Good Night For Dreaming"
585 "Judy's An Angel"/"Baggy Pants" 1961
610 "Don't Fly Away"/"Julie"

Challenge
9111 "Heart And Soul"/"Those Words" 1961
9111 "Heart And Soul"/"Midsummer's Nights Dream"
9120 "Wanted: One Girl"/"Something A Little Bit Different"

Liberty
55397 "A Sunday Kind Of Love"/"Poor Little Puppet" 1962
55454 "Tennessee"/"Your Heart Has Changed Its Mind"
55496 "Who Put The Bomp"/"My Favorite Dream"
55522 "She's Still Talkin' Baby Talk"/"Frosty The Snowman"

55531 "Linda"/"When I Learn How To Cry" 1963
55580 "Surf City"/"She's My Summer Girl"
55613 "Honolulu Lulu"/"Someday"
55641 "Drag City"/"Schlock Rod Part 1"
55672 "Dead Man's Curve"/"New Girl In School" 1964
55704 "The Little Old Lady From Pasadena"/"My Mighty G.T.O."
55724 "Ride The Wild Surf"/"The Anaheim, Azusa And Cucamonga Sewing Circle, Book Review And Timing Association"
55727 "Sidewalk Surfin'"/"When It's Over"
55766 "From All Over The World"/"Freeway Flyer" 1965
55792 "You Really Know How To Hurt A Guy"/"It's As Easy As 1-2-3"
55833 "I Found A Girl"/"It's A Shame To Say Goodbye"

As by Jan Berry:

Liberty
55845 "The Universal Coward"/"I Can't Wait To Love You"

As by Jan And Dean:

Liberty
55849 "Folk City"/"A Beginning From An End" 1966
55860 "Batman"/"Bucket 'T'"
55866 "Popsicle"/"Norwegian Wood"
55905 "Fiddle Around"/"Surfer's Dream"
55923 "School Days"/"New Girl In School"

Jan And Dean
10 "Hawaii"/"Tijuana" 1965
11 "Fan Tan"/"Love & Hate"
401 "California Lullabye"/"Summertime Summertime" 1966
402 "Louisiana Man"/"Like A Summer Rain"

Columbia
44036 "Yellow Balloon"/"Taste Of Rain" 1967

Warner Brothers
7151 "Only A Boy"/"Love & Hate" 1967
7219 "Laurel & Hardy"/"I Know My Mind" 1968

THE BEACH BOYS

The Beach Boys were the innovators and the prime exponents of the surf rock/hot rod rock school so popular during the very early 60's. The on-target title lyric of "Surfin'" was a perfect representation of the California life style. Other West Coast portrayals include "California Girls" and "Be True To Your School," as well as the teen-themed "Fun, Fun, Fun" and "I Get Around." The Beach Boys had a charm and a polish which brought great success to this bright California rock and roll sound.

Values

The original X label version of the mild Los Angeles area hit "Surfin'" reached the inflated price of $50 in recent record auctions. Realistically, "Surfin'" on X is valued around $20, while the Candix reissue is a solid $5 record. Most of the Capitol singles are in the $2 to $3 area. Two Capitol label 45's which are scarce and in demand are "Ten Little Indians" and "The Man With All The Toys," worth, perhaps, $5.

Discography

As by The Beach Boys:

X
301 "Surfin'"/"Luau" (also on Candix 301) 1962

Capitol

4777	"Surfin' Safari"/"409"	1962
4880	"Ten Little Indians"/"County Fair" (also on Capitol 6060)	1963
4932	"Surfin' U.S.A."/"Shut Down"	
5009	"Surfer Girl"/"Little Deuce Coupe"	
----	"Boogie Woogie"/"Spirit Of America" (special promotion issue, no record #)	
5069	"Be True To Your School"/"In My Room"	
5096	"Little Saint Nick"/"The Lord's Prayer"	
5118	"Fun, Fun, Fun"/"Why Do Fools Fall In Love"	1964
5174	"I Get Around"/"Don't Worry Baby"	
5245	"When I Grow Up"/"She Knows Me Too Well"	
5267	"Little Honda"/"Wendy"/"Hushabye"/ "Don't Look Back"	
5306	"Dance Dance Dance"/"The Warmth Of The Sun"	
5312	"The Man With All The Toys"/"Blue Christmas"	
5372	"Do You Wanna Dance"/"Please Let Me Wonder"	1965
5395	"Help Me Rhonda"/"Kiss Me Baby"	
5464	"California Girls"/"Let Him Run Wild"	
5540	"Little Girl I Once Knew"/"There's No Other"	
5561	"Barbara Ann"/"Girl Don't Tell Me"	
5602	"Sloop John B"/"You're So Good To Me"	1966

As by Brian Wilson:

Capitol

5610	"Caroline No"/"Summer Means New Love"	1966

As by The Beach Boys:

Capitol		
5676	"Good Vibrations"/"Let's Go Away For Awhile"	1966
5706	"God Only Knows"/"Wouldn't It Be Nice"	
2028	"Wild Honey"/"Wind Chimes"	1967
2068	"Darlin'"/"Here Today"	
2160	"Friends"/"Little Bird"	1968
2239	"Do It Again"/"Wake The World"	
2360	"Bluebirds Over The Mountain"/"Never Learn Not To Love"	
2432	"I Can Hear Music"/"All I Want To Do"	1969
2530	"Break Away"/"Celebrate The News"	
Brother		
1001	"Heroes And Villains"/"You're Welcome"	1967
1002	"Gettin' Hungry"/"Devoted To You"	

ANNETTE

A graduate of TV's *Mickey Mouse Club*, Annette Funicello's first record was released while she was still a teen mouse clubber. The record on the Disneyland label was entitled "How Will I Know My Love." This particular title became a real Annette standby, appearing as the flip of two later Annette singles. Her first hit was "Tall Paul," a likable song about her high school sweetheart. Other hits had, again, to do with her boyfriend, in "First Name Initial," and with Annette as a hula dancer in "Pineapple Princess." Annette's popularity coincided with that of The Beach Boys and their backing can be heard in her 1963 single "The Monkey's Uncle."

Values

Few of Annette's 45 RPM singles on both Disneyland and Vista, even with picture sleeves, bring more than $2. The exception is "The Monkey's Uncle," which features vocal backing by The Beach Boys and can fetch $5.

Discography

Disneyland

758 "How Will I Know My Love"/"Annette" (by Jimmy Dodd) 1959
102 "Don't Jump To Conclusions"/"How Will I Know My Love"
118 "Tall Paul"/"Ma—He's Making Eyes At Me"

Buena Vista

336 "Lonely Guitar"/"Jo Jo The Dog Faced Boy" 1959
339 "Lonely Guitar"/"Wild Willie"
349 "First Name Initial"/"My Heart Became Of Age"
354 "O Dio Mio"/"I Took Dreams" 1960
359 "Train Of Love"/"Tell Me Who's The Girl"
362 "Pineapple Princess"/"Luau Cha Cha Cha"
369 "Talk To Me Baby"/"I Love You Baby" 1961
374 "Dream Boy"/"Please Please Signore"
384 "Blue Muu Muu"/"Hawaiian Love Talk"
802 "Theme From The Parent Trap"/"Let's Get Together" (with Tommy Sands)
388 "Dreamin' About You"/"Strummin' Song" 1962
392 "That Crazy Place In Outer Space"/"Seven Moon" (by Dany Saval & Tom Tryon)
394 "Truth About Youth"/"I Can't Do The Sum"
405 "Mr. Piano Man"/"He's My Ideal"
414 "Teenage Wedding"/"Walkin' And Talkin'"

427 "Treat Him Nicely"/"Promise Me Anything" 1963
431 "The Scrambled Egghead"/"Merlin Jones"
432 "Custom City"/"Rebel Rider"
433 "Muscle Beach Party"/"I Dream About Frankie"
436 "Bikini Beach Party"/"The Clyde"
437 "The Wah Watusi"/"The Clyde"
438 "How Will I Know My Love"
440 "The Monkey's Uncle"/"How Will I Know My Love"
442 "Boy To Love"/"No One Else Could Be Prouder"
450 "No Way To Go But Up"/"Crystal Ball"

Pacific Northwest Rock and Roll

◉

The Pacific Northwest was the spawning ground for the exciting early 60's rock and roll sound of such mainly instrumental groups as The Wailers and The Sonics, as well as such instrumental and vocal groups as Paul Revere And The Raiders, The Kingsmen and Don And The Goodtimes. The Northwest sound featured a strong guitar beat, and was a predecessor to the psychedelic hard rock sound popular in the late 60's.

PAUL REVERE AND THE RAIDERS

Paul Revere And The Raiders were a first-generation 60's rock and roll group, the most successful of the several Pacific Northwest rock groups. The bulk of their "Like . . ." titles for the small Gardena label of Los Angeles were competent rock and roll instrumentals. With Columbia, The Raiders at first concentrated on rendering well-known rhythm and blues standards. However, Paul Revere And The

Raiders became the first Columbia label hard rock group only after release of an original hit, "Steppin' Out." The hard-core best of Paul Revere's power-packed rock were four singles: "Steppin' Out," "Just Like Me," "Kicks" (which was against hard drugs) and "Hungry," all issued in 1965 and 1966. These four singles were the pinnacle of success for this very capable rock and roll unit, though they continued to record sporadic hits for the rest of the 60's.

Values

The most sought-after Paul Revere And The Raiders singles are those released on the Gardena label, a small concern that distributed mainly in the western United States. These Gardena label 45's can bring at least $5, as can the earliest Columbia singles (up to Columbia 43272), together with the special Camaro issue on Columbia CSM 466. Many of the hit singles by Paul Revere And The Raiders are worth under $2, even with picture sleeves.

Discography

Gardena

106	"Beatnick Sticks"/"Orbit (The Spy)"	1960
115	"Paul Revere's Ride"/"Unfinished Fifth"	
116	"Like Long Hair"/"Sharon"	1961
118	"Like Charleston"/"Midnite Ride"	
124	"All Night Long"	
127	"Like Bluegrass"/"Leatherneck"	1962
131	"Shake It Up"	
137	"Tall Cool One"/"Road Runner"	

Jerden

807	"So Fine"/"Blues Stay Away"	

Columbia

42814	"Louie Louie"/"Night Train"	1963
43008	"Have Love Will Travel"/"Louie Go Home"	1964
43114	"Over You"/"Swim"	
43272	"Oo Poo Pah Doo"/"Sometimes"	
43375	"Steppin' Out"/"Blue Fox"	1965
43461	"Just Like Me"/"B.F.D.R.F. Blues"	
43556	"Kicks"/"Shake It Up"	
43678	"Hungry"/"There She Goes"	1966
43810	"The Great Airplane Strike"/"In My Community"	
43907	"Good Thing"/"Undecided Man"	
44018	"Ups And Downs"/"Leslie"	1967
44094	"Him Or Me—What's It Gonna Be"/ "Legend Of Paul Revere"	
44227	"I Had A Dream"/"Upon Your Leaving"	
44262	"Corvair Baby"/"SS 396"	

CSM

466	"SS 396"/"Camaro" (by The Cyrcle)	
44335	"Peace Of Mind"/"Do Unto Others"	
44444	"Happening 68"/"Too Much Talk"	1968
44553	"Don't Take It So Hard"/"Observation From Flight 285"	
44655	"Cinderella Sunshine"/"Theme From What's Happening"	
44744	"Mr. Sun, Mr. Moon"/"Without You"	1969
44854	"Let Me"/"I Don't Know"	
44970	"We Gotta Get It All Together"/ "Frankfort Side Street"	
45082	"Sorceress With Blue Eyes"/"Just Seventeen"	

THE WAILERS

The Wailers were among the best of several Pacific Northwest rock and roll instrumental groups. The powerful guitar work in the tightly performed

"Tall Cool One" created not only a hit for The Wailers but a best seller for a period of several years. Though not as successful, later releases were every bit as good as "Tall Cool One." In particular, "Dirty Robber" was a gritty, rocking vocal.

Values

Singles by The Wailers on Golden Crest can bring from $2 to $3.

Discography

Golden Crest

518	"Tall Cool One"/"Road Runner"	1961
526	"Mau Mau"/"Dirty Robber"	1962
532	"Shanghaied"/"Wailin'"	
545	"Lucille"/"Scratchin'"	
591	"Beat Guitar"	1963

Etiquette

2	"Mashi"/"Vela"	
6	"We're Goin' Surfin'"/"Shakedown"	1963
21	"Out Of Our Tree"/"I Got Me"	1965

Imperial

66045	"On The Rocks"/"Mashi"	1964

THE KINGSMEN

The sound of The Kingsmen had all the charm of a clanging hubcap. Yet "Louie Louie," borrowed from the Richard Berry classic composition, was a thumping success. The Northwest instrumental-vocal unit had a primitive sound, ideal for such hard-hitting rhythm and blues material as Barrett Strong's "Money" and Donald Woods's "Death Of An Angel."

Compositions original to The Kingsmen in the mid-60's were largely topical with such novelty lyrics as "The Jolly Green Giant" and "Annie Fanny," both hits.

Values

Single releases by The Kingsmen on the Wand label are not in consistent demand and thus the price level is well below $2.

Discography

Wand

143	"Louie Louie"/"Haunted Castle"	1963
150	"Money"/"Bent Scepter"	1964
157	"Little Latin Lupe Lu"/"David's Mood"	
164	"Death Of An Angel"/"Searching For Love"	
172	"The Jolly Green Giant"/"Long Green"	1965
183	"The Climb"/"I'm Waiting"	
189	"Annie Fanny"/"Give Her Lovin'"	
1107	"It's Only The Dog"/"The Gamma Goochee"	
1115	"Killer Joe"/"Little Green Thing"	1966
1127	"My Wife Can't Cook"/"Little Sally Tease"	
1137	"The Grass Is Green"/"I Need Someone"	
1154	"The Wolf Of Manhattan"/"Children's Caretaker"	
1174	"Get Out Of My Life Woman"	
1180	"I Guess I Was Dreamin'"/"On Love"	

Rockabilly Roots II: Early 60's Rock and Roll

Traces of rockabilly were evident in the work of several of the biggest names during the pre-Beatles 60's rock and roll. Buddy Holly was the unmistakable influence in the early work of Tommy Roe, Bobby Fuller, Jimmy Gilmer, and Bobby Vee, while Johnny Tillotson borrowed heavily from Hank Williams and Ral Donner drew upon the approach, style and even vocal inflections of Elvis Presley.

JIMMY CLANTON

Jimmy Clanton's earliest success was with the flatly rendered ballad, "Just A Dream." The record was nicely set off through vigorous rhythm and blues instrumental work. Other hits for Jimmy Clanton were the late 50's releases, "My Own True Love," done in medium tempo, along with the more danceable "Go Jimmy Go." In 1962, Jimmy Clanton had his biggest hit, the glossy, pop-styled "Venus In Blue Jeans."

Values

Jimmy Clanton's earliest releases on the now-defunct Ace label average $2 to $3, especially with picture sleeves.

Discography

Ace		
537	"I Trusted You"/"That's You Baby"	1958
546	"Just A Dream"/"You Aim To Please"	
551	"Letter To An Angel"/"A Part Of Me"	
560	"Ship On A Stormy Sea"/"My Love Is Strong"	1959
567	"My Own True Love"/"Little Boy In Love"	
575	"Go Jimmy Go"/"I Trusted You"	
585	"Another Sleepless Night"/"I'm Gonna Try"	1960
600	"Come Back"/"Wait"	
607	"What Am I Gonna Do"/"Am I"	1961
616	"Down The Aisle"/"No Longer Blue" (with Mary Ann Mobley)	
622	"Don't Look At Me"/"I Just Wanna Make Love"	
634	"Lucky In Love With You"/"Not Like A Brother"	
641	"Twist On Little Girl"/"Wayward Girl"	1962
8001	"Venus In Blue Jeans"/"Highway Bound"	
8005	"Darkest Street In Town"/"Dreams Of A Fool"	1963
8006	"Endless Nights"	
8007	"Cindy"/"I Care Enough"	
Imperial		
66274	"I'll Be Loving You"/"Calico Junction"	1965

JOHNNY TILLOTSON

Johnny Tillotson gave promise of becoming a major rock and roll talent based on his first few single releases. Tillotson's initial Cadence label recording was the flashy, quick-tempo "Well, I'm Your Man." Johnny Tillotson's countrified voice gave an unusual quality to his renderings of some well-known rhythm and blues love songs, in particular, Johnny Ace's "Never Let Me Go" and "Pledging My Love," along with the flip "Earth Angel," the Penguins' standard. "Dreamy Eyes" was a twice-released major ballad success for Johnny Tillotson.

His biggest sellers were the slick rocker "Poetry In Motion" in 1961 and the melancholy "It Keeps Right On A-Hurtin'" in 1962. Johnny Tillotson had no major hits after 1962, though he did receive some attention with the remakes of the Hank Williams evergreens "Send Me The Pillow You Dream On," "I Can't Help It" and "I'm So Lonesome I Could Cry," which coincided with a brief early 60's Hank Williams revival.

Values

Johnny Tillotson's releases on Cadence, especially his hit issues, fetch $2 or less.

Discography

Cadence

1353	"Well, I'm Your Man"/"Dreamy Eyes" (reissued on Cadence 1409)	1958
1365	"True True Happiness"/"Love Is Blind"	1959
1372	"Why Do I Love You So"/"Never Let Me Go"	

1377	"Pledging My Love"/"Earth Angel"	1960
1384	"Poetry In Motion"/"Princess, Princess"	
1391	"Jimmy's Girl"/"His True Love Said Goodbye"	1961
1404	"Without You"/"Cutie Pie"	
1418	"It Keeps Right On A-Hurtin'"/"She Gave Sweet Love To Me"	1962
1424	"Send Me The Pillow You Dream On"/ "What'll I Do"	
1432	"I'm So Lonesome I Could Cry"/"I Can't Help It"	
1434	"Out Of My Mind"/"Empty Feelin'"	1963
1437	"You Can Never Stop Me Loving You"/ "Judy, Judy, Judy"	
1441	"Funny How Time Slips Away"/"A Very Good Year For Girls"	

BOBBY VEE/TOMMY ROE

The recording careers of Bobby Vee and Tommy Roe suggest interesting parallels. Both men began their careers with tiny regional record labels. They switched to majors by virtue of having their earliest hit singles re-released by a major. Bobby Vee's "Suzy Baby" was transferred from Soma to Liberty, while Tommy Roe's "Sheila" went from Judd to ABC. "Suzy Baby" and "Sheila" both rocked with a dominant guitar beat borrowed heavily from Buddy Holly's bigger-than-life hit record, "Peggy Sue."

However, it was soon apparent that the developing sound of 60's rock and roll was not the hard edge of Southern rockabilly, rather it was to be a much softer pop sound. During this period of transition, Bobby Vee and Tommy Roe opted for this easygoing pop rock and roll approach—this gave their recordings enormous teen appeal.

BOBBY VEE

Bobby Vee began his recording career with The Shadows back-up band while on the small Minnesota Soma label. While Bobby Vee performed on the road, fellow Minnesotan Bob Dylan was in his band for a short period of time, though probably he isn't heard on any recording sessions. "Suzy Baby," a simple, unpretentious rocker, was a minor hit on Liberty. The flip to "Suzy Baby," entitled "Flying Home," is an excellent rockabilly instrumental with strong Link Wray/Duane Eddy influences. Bobby Vee then turned to more pop material, yet with remaining rockabilly and Holly influences in "Everyday" and "More Than I Can Say"—Vee used Holly's cracking vocal inflections in each.

For a while in the early 60's, it appeared that Bobby Vee was trying to fill some of the void left after Holly's 1959 death. Vee actually recorded with The Crickets. However, "What Do You Want" and "Devil Or Angel," a remake of a Clovers classic, gave evidence of a new, more subdued pop style. Bobby Vee found his greatest success with this highly commercial form through the popish upbeat "Rubber Ball" in 1960, "Take Good Care Of My Baby" in 1961 and his last early 60's hit, "The Night Has A Thousand Eyes" in 1962. In 1967, Bobby Vee reappeared with two more best sellers, the appealing ballad, "Come Back When You Grow Up" and the very topical "Beautiful People."

Values

Bobby Vee's first effort on the Soma label can fetch from $3 to $5, while the Liberty reissue is in a slightly lower $2 to $3 bracket. The bulk of the Liberty label singles only bring $2, even when with picture sleeves.

Discography

As by Bobby Vee And The Shadows:

Soma

1110 "Suzy Baby"/"Flyin' High" 1959

Liberty

55204 "Suzy Baby"/"Flyin' High"

As by Bobby Vee:

Liberty

55234 "What Do You Want"/"My Baby Loves Me" 1960
55251 "Laurie"/"One Last Kiss"
55270 "Devil Or Angel"/"Since I Met You Baby"
55287 "Rubber Ball"/"Everyday"
55296 "Stayin' In"/"More Than I Can Say" 1961
55325 "How Many Tears"/"Baby Face"
55354 "Take Good Care Of My Baby"/"Bashful Bob"
55388 "Run To Him"/"Walkin' With My Angel"
55419 "Please Don't Ask About Barbara"/"I Can't Say Goodbye" 1962
55451 "Sharing You"/"In My Baby's Eyes"

As by Bobby Vee And The Crickets:

Liberty

55479 "Punish Her"/"Someday" 1962

As by Bobby Vee:

Liberty

55521 "The Night Has A Thousand Eyes"/"Anonymous Phone Call"
55530 "Charms"/"Bobby Tomorrow" 1963
55581 "Be True To Yourself"/"A Letter From Betty"

55636 "Yesterday And You"/"Never Love A Robin"
55654 "Stranger In Your Arms"/"1963"
55670 "I'll Make You Mine"/"She's Sorry" 1964
55700 "Hickory Dick And Doc"/"I Wish You Were Mine Again"
55726 "Where Is She"/"How To Make A Farewell"
55751 "Pretend You Don't See Her"/"Ev'ry Little Bit Hurts"
55761 "Cross My Heart"/"This Is The End"
55790 "Keep On Trying"/"You Want To Forget Me"
55828 "Run Like The Devil"/"Take A Look Around Me"
55843 "The Story Of My Life"/"High Coin"
55854 "Gone"/"A Girl I Used To Know"
55877 "Butterfly"/"Save A Love" (alternate title) 1966
55921 "Before You Go"/"Here Today"
55964 "Come Back When You Grow Up"/ "Swahili Serenade" or "That's All In The Past" (alternate titles) 1967
55964 "Come Back Before You Grow Up"/"That's All In The Past" (alternate title)
56009 "Beautiful People"/"I May Be Gone"
56014 "Maybe Just Today"/"You're A Big Girl Now"
56033 "Medley: My Girl—Hey Girl"/"Just Keep It Up" 1968
56057 "Do What You Gotta Do"/"Thank You"
56080 "Someone To Love Me"/"Thank You"
56096 "Santa Cruz"/"Jenny Came To Mc" 1969
56124 "Let's Call It A Day Girl"
56149 "Electric Trains And You"/"In And Out Of Love"

TOMMY ROE

Tommy Roe's original releases for the Judd label,

"Caveman" and "Sheila," were both strong rockers. Later releases by Tommy Roe, including "Sweet Pea" and "Carol" (borrowed from Chuck Berry) were certainly rock and roll, but an infinitely more subdued rock and roll. By 1966, Tommy Roe had crossed over to an ultraglossy bubble gum approach with the flowerly, innocent singles, "Hooray For Hazel" in 1966, "Little Miss Sunshine" in 1967, and two monster 1969 hits, "Dizzy" and "Jam Up And Jelly Tight."

Values

Tommy Roe's "Caveman" on the Judd label is worth $5 or more, while "Sheila," also on Judd, is considerably scarcer, and brings from $15 to $20. The remake of "Sheila" and the next four ABC label singles (to ABC 10454) are in the $2 to $3 range, especially with picture sleeves. Later ABC issues by Tommy Roe are well below $2.

Discography

Judd

1018	"Caveman"/"I Gotta Girl"	1959
1022	"Sheila"/"Pretty Girl"	

ABC

10329	"Sheila"/"Share Your Kisses"	1962
10362	"Susie Darlin'"/"Piddle De Pat"	
10379	"Town Crier"/"Rainbow"	
10389	"Don't Cry Donna"/"Gonna Take A Chance"	1963
10423	"The Folk Singer"/"Count On Me"	
10454	"Kiss And Run"/"What Makes The Blues"	
10478	"Everybody"/"Sorry I'm Late, Lisa"	
10515	"Come On"/"There Will Be Better Years"	1964
10543	"Carol"/"Be A Good Little Girl"	

10555	"Dance With Me Henry"/"Wild Water Skiing Weekend"	
10579	"Oh So Right"/"I Think I Love You"	
10604	"Party Girl"/"Oh How I Could Love You"	1965
10665	"Fourteen Pairs Of Shoes"/"Combo Music"	
10706	"I Keep Remembering"/"Wish You Didn't Have To Go"	
10738	"Every Time A Bluebird Cries"/"Doesn't Anybody Know My Name"	
10762	"Sweet Pea"/"Much More Love"	1966
10852	"Hooray For Hazel"/"Need Your Love"	
10888	"It's Now Winter's Days"/"Kick Me Charlie"	
10908	"Sing Along With Me"/"Nightime"	1967
10945	"Little Miss Sunshine"/"The You I Need"	
10989	"Paisley Dream"/"Melancholy Moon"	
11039	"Soft Words"/"Dottie I Like It"	
11076	"Sugar Cane"/"An Oldie But Goodie"	
11140	"Gotta Keep Rolling Along"/"It's Gonna Hurt Me"	1968
11164	"Dizzy"/"The You I Need"	
11211	"Heather Honey"/"Money Is My Pay"	1969
11229	"Jack & Jill"/"Tip Toe Tina"	
11247	"Jam Up Jelly Tight"/"Moontalk"	
11258	"Firefly"/"Stir It Up And Serve It"	
11266	"Pearl"/"Dollar's Worth Of Pennies"	

THE FIREBALLS

The Fireballs began as a first-class instrumental rock and roll combo. "Torquay" and "Bull Dog" were uncomplicated guitar performances that gave The Fireballs two best selling hits. A Texas group, The Fireballs then had few hits until the release of the Jimmy Gilmer vocal of "Sugar Shack." Gilmer's vocal ability was lackluster, yet "Sugar Shack" was a pleasant, restrained rock and roll hit. The next Dot label release, "Daisy Petal Pickin'," also sold well. The Fireballs coasted until 1969, when they brought out—this time on Atco—the folk-influenced rockers "Come On React!" and "Bottle Of Wine."

Values

The Fireballs recorded some excellent rock and roll instrumentals on both the Top Rank and Warwick labels. These 45 RPM singles generally bring about $2. Later releases, with Jimmy Gilmer featured as a vocalist, although good sellers, do not approach the demand or price for earlier instrumental efforts.

Discography

As by The Fireballs:

Top Rank

2008	"Torquay"/"Cry Baby"	1959
2026	"Bull Dog"/"Nearly Sunrise"	1960
2038	"Kissin'"/"Foot Patter"	
2054	"Vacquero"/"Chief Whoopin-Koff"	
2081	"Almost Paradise"/"Sweet Talk"	
3003	"Rik A Tik"/"Yacky Doo"	1961

Warwick

502	"Good Good Lovin'"/"Do You Think"	
547	"True Love Ways"/"Wishing"	
630	"Rik-A-Tik"/"Yacky Doo"	1961
644	"Quite A Party"/"Gunshot"	

Dot

16493	"Torquay Two"/"Peg Leg"	1963
16661	"Dumbo"	
16715	"More Than I Can Say"/"Beating Of My Heart"	1964

16745	"Ahhh Soul"/"Campusology"	
16834	"La-Da"/"What Am I"	
16881	"Ain't That Rain"/"All I Do Is Dream Of You"	

As by Jimmy Gilmer And The Fireballs:

Dot

16487	"Sugar Shack"/"My Heart Is Free"	1963
16539	"Daisy Petal Pickin'"/"When My Tears Have Dried"	
16583	"Ain't Gonna Tell Anybody"/"Young I Am"	1964
16609	"Look At Me"	
16642	"Wishing"/"What Kinda Love"	
16666	"Thunder And Lightning"	
16714	"Lonesome Tears"/"Born To Be With You"	1964
16743	"Fool"/"Somebody Stole My Watermelon"	
16768	"Codine"/"Come To Me"	
16786	"She Belongs To Me"/"Ramblers Blues"	
16833	"Hungry, Hungry, Hungry"/"White Roses"	1965

Atco

6491	"Bottle Of Wine"/"Can't You See I'm Tryin'"	1967
6569	"Goin' Away"/"Groovy Motions"	1968
6595	"Chicken Little"/"3 Minutes Time"	
6641	"Come On React!"/"Woman, Help Me!"	
6651	"Long Green"/"Light In The Window"	1969

RAL DONNER

Ral Donner was the most successful of the several late 50's Elvis Presley sound-alikes. Ral Donner's appeal went beyond his similarity to Elvis, he recorded some fine and original rock and roll. Donner's basic theme was that of unrequited love, found in both "Girl Of My Best Friend," his biggest hit which was recorded earlier by none other than Elvis Presley, and his fine follow-up release "You Don't Know What You Got Until You Lose It." These melancholy recordings were rendered in an intensely moody, uptempo style.

Values

Singles by Ral Donner on the Gone label were generally hits and thus bring only $2 or $3. Later, more obscure issues on Reprise and especially Fontana and Red Bird are quite scarce and can bring over $5 from a die-hard collector of Ral Donner.

Discography

Gone

5102	"Girl Of My Best Friend"/"It's Been A Long Long Time"	1961
5108	"You Don't Know What You've Got Until You Lose It"/"So Close To Heaven"	
5114	"I Didn't Figure On Him"/"Please Don't Go"	
5119	"School Of Heartbreakers"/"Because We're Young"	
5121	"She's Everything"/"Will You Love Me In Heaven"	
5121	"She's Everything"/"Because We're Young"	
5125	"To Love Somebody"/"Will You Love Me In Heaven"	1962
5129	"Loveless Life"/"Bells Of Love"	
5133	"To Love"/"Sweetheart"	

MJ

222	"Lovin' Place"/"My Heart Sings"	

Reprise
- 0135 "Second Miracle"
- 0141 "I Got Burned"/"A Tear In My Eye" 1963
- 0176 "I Wish This Night Would Never End"
- 0192 "Run Little Linda"/"Beyond The Heartbreak"

Fontana
- 1502 "Poison Ivy League"/"Tear In My Eye" 1964
- 1515 "Good Lovin' "/"Other Side Of Me"

Red Bird
- 10051 "Love Isn't Like That"/"It Will Only Make You Love Me More" 1965

DEL SHANNON

Del Shannon's two best sellers, "Runaway" and "Hats Off To Larry," were strident, pleading rock and roll vocals. Many of Del Shannon's follow-up releases on Big Top were also good sellers, yet Shannon's next major hit was an Amy label release, the rocking "Keep Searchin'."

Values

Singles by Del Shannon on Big Top and Berlee can bring $2, while issues on Amy bring well under that.

Discography

Big Top
- 3067 "Runaway"/"Jody" 1961
- 3075 "Hats Off To Larry"/"Don't Gild The Lily Lily"
- 3083 "So Long Baby"/"The Answer To Everything"
- 3091 "Hey Little Girl"/"I Don't Care Anymore"

3098 "I Won't Be There"/"Ginny In The Mirror" 1962
3112 "Cry Myself To Sleep"/"I'm Gonna Move On"
3117 "The Swiss Maid"/"You Never Talked About Me"
3131 "Little Town Flirt"/"The Wamboo" 1963
3143 "Two Kinds Of Teardrops"/"Kelly"
3152 "From Me To You"/"Two Silhouettes"

Berlee
501 "Sue's Gotta Be Mine"/"Now That She's Gone" 1963
502 "That's The Way Love Is"/"Time Of The Day"

Amy
897 "Mary Jane"/"Stains On My Letter" 1964
905 "Handy Man"/"Give Her Lots Of Lovin'"
913 "Do You Wanna Dance"/"This Is All I Have To Give" 1965
915 "Keep Searchin'"/"Broken Promises"
919 "Stranger In Town"/"Over You"
925 "Break Up"/"Why Don't You Tell Him" 1966
937 "Move It On Over"/"She Still Remembers Tony"

Liberty
55866 "The Big Hurt"/"I Got It Bad" 1965
55889 "For A Little While"/"Hey Little Star" 1966
55894 "Show Me"/"Never Thought I Could"
55904 "Under My Thumb"/"She Was Mine"
55939 "She"/"What Makes You Run"
55961 "Led Along"/"I Can't Be True" 1967
55993 "Runaway"/"He Cheated"
56018 "Thinkin' It Over"/"Runnin' On Back"
56036 "Gemini"/"Magical Musical Box" 1968
56070 "Raindrops"/"You Don't Love Me"

Dunhill

4193	"Come Back To Me"/"Sweet Mary Lou"	1969
4224	"Sister Isabelle"/"Colorado Rain"	

JOHNNY RIVERS

Johnny Rivers was a consistently popular mid-60's discotheque "a-go-go" rock and roll artist. His earliest Imperial label releases were upbeat, brisk performances of rock and roll standards: Chuck Berry's "Memphis" and "Maybellene," as well as "Moody River." The latter was an early 60's Pat Boone hit —a cover record taken from the 50's champion cover artist no less, no doubt a first! Johnny Rivers also recorded one fine hit original composition entitled "Secret Agent Man," taken from a popular TV series. These rock and roll recordings all had a "live" sound, and each was a hit.

However, the strongest performances by Johnny Rivers were introspective folk ballads, "Poor Side Of Town" and "Summer Rain." Johnny Rivers also hit with some Motown-composed soul music hits, "Baby I Need Your Lovin'," a Four Tops original, and "The Tracks Of My Tears," a best seller for The Miracles. His last 60's releases dealt with then fashionable alternate life styles in the flowery "Going Back To Big Sur," "Jesus Was A Soul Man" and "Into The Mystic." However, Johnny Rivers's greatest success was as a proponent of diverting, danceable rock and roll.

Values

Recordings by Johnny Rivers on the small Dee Dee label, as well as each of his early releases—on Cub, Guyden, Chancellor and on Era—bring some $3. Even early issues on Imperial were major hits and thus bring under $2, with picture sleeves.

Discography

Cub		
9047	"Everyday"/"Darling Talk To Me"	1959
Dee Dee		
239	"Your First And Last Love"/"That's My Babe" (also on Coral 62425)	ca. 1960
Era		
3037	"Andersonville"/"Call Me"	1960
Guyden		
2033	"You're The One"/"Hole In The Ground"	1962
Chancellor		
1070	"Knock Three Times"/"I Get So Doggone Lonesome"	
1096	"Blue Skies"	1962
1108	"To Be Loved"/"Too Good To Last"	
Imperial		
66032	"Memphis"/"It Wouldn't Happen To Me"	1964
66056	"Maybellene"/"Walk Myself On Home"	
66075	"Moody River"/"Mountain Of Love"	
66087	"Midnight Special"/"Cupid"	1965
66112	"Seventh Son"/"Un-Square Dance"	
66133	"Where Have All The Flowers Gone"/"Love Me While You Can"	
66144	"Under Your Spell Again"/"Long Time Man"	
66159	"Secret Agent Man"/"You Dig"	1966
66175	"Muddy Water"/"Roogalator"	
66205	"Poor Side Of Town"/"A Man Can Cry"	
66227	"Baby I Need Your Lovin'"/"Gettin' Ready For Tomorrow"	1967
66244	"The Tracks Of My Tears"/"Rewind Medley"	
66267	"Summer Rain"/"Memory Of The Coming Good"	

66286	"Look To Your Soul"/"Something Strange"	1968
66335	"Right Relations"/"A Better Life"	
66360	"Going Back To Big Sur"/"These Are Not My People"	
66386	"Muddy River"/"Resurrection"	1969
66418	"Ode To John Lee"/"One Woman"	
66448	"Into The Mystic"/"Jesus Was A Soul Man"	

THE BOBBY FULLER 4

Bobby Fuller has been compared to the legendary Buddy Holly. Parallels have been drawn to the Texas origin of each, as well as the untimely death of each man. Some imply that when Buddy Holly and Bobby Fuller died, they were somehow on the threshold of rock and roll superstardom. Fuller's first record on the small Southwest Yucca label was an excellent example of early 60's rockabilly, by then a dying form. Bobby Fuller did not have a hit until his association with the Los Angeles Mustang label, for whom he recorded the moderately rebellious "I Fought The Law (And The Law Won)." One of Fuller's later releases was a rendition of Buddy Holly's "Love's Made A Fool Of You." The recordings by The Bobby Fuller 4 do reveal a potent rock and roll talent, yet the quantity of work released is disappointingly limited.

Values

Singles by Bobby Fuller on both Yucca and Donna were quite poor sellers and now are valued up to $5 by dedicated Fuller collectors. His Mustang label issues were considerably more popular, especially on the West Coast, and generally bring $2 or $3.

Discography

As by Bobby Fuller:

Yucca

144	"My Heart Jumped"/"Gently My Love"	ca. 1961

Todd

1090	"Saturday Night"	

Donna

1403	"Those Memories Of You"/"Our Favorite Martian"	1964

As by The Bobby Fuller 4:

Mustang

3004	"She's My Girl"/"Take My Word"	1964
3006	"Let Her Dance"/"Another Sad And Lonely Night"	1965
3011	"You Kiss Me"/"Never To Be Forgotten"	
3014	"I Fought The Law"/"Little Annie Lou" (also on Liberty 55812)	
3016	"Love's Made A Fool Out Of You"/"Don't Ever Leave Me"	1966
3018	"The Magic Touch"/"My True Love"	

LOU CHRISTIE

Lou Christie's high-pitched vocal delivery gave his pouting rock and roll enormous appeal. Lou Christie's themes were constant, the emotions of rejected love found in two 1963 successes: "The Gypsy Cried" and "Two Faces Have I." This energy-charged approach was evident in two of his MGM label hits, "Lightning Strikes" and the controversial "Rhapsody In The Rain," best described as orgasm rock. "Rhapsody In The Rain" was the focal point of a mid-60's revival of suppression directed at both drug and sexually-oriented rock and roll recordings. Lou Christie, although an unlikely candidate, became an idol for young teen girls during the early 60's, he proffered them highly emotional experiences which they could readily accept.

Values

Lou Christie recorded for an unusually high number of labels, rarely with more than four or five singles on any label. Most of Lou Christie's earlier releases are worth $2, slightly more with picture sleeves. Later issues are not as sought-after, which keeps the value below $2.

Discography

Roulette

4457	"The Gypsy Cried"/"Red Sails In The Sunset"	1963
4481	"Two Faces Have I"/"All That Glitters Isn't Gold"	
4504	"How Many Teardrops"/"You And I"	1964
4527	"Shy Boy"/"It Can Happen"	
4545	"There They Go"/"Stay"	
4554	"When You Dance"/"Maybe You'll Be There"	

American Music Makers

006	"The Jury"/"Little Did I Know"	

MGM

13412	"Lightning Strikes"/"Cryin' In The Streets"	1965
13473	"Rhapsody In The Rain"/"Trapeze"	1966

13533	"Painter"/"Du Ronda"	
13623	"Since I Don't Have You"/"Wild Life's Season"	

Colpix

735	"Merry-Go-Round"/"Guitars And Bongos"	1965
753	"Have I Sinned"/"Pot Of Gold"	
770	"Make Summer Last Forever"	
799	"Big Time"/"Crying On My Knees"	1966

Co & Ce

235	"Outside The Gates Of Heaven"/"All That Glitters Isn't Gold"	1966

Columbia

44062	"Shake Hands And Walk Away Crying"/"Escape"	1967
44177	"Self Expression"/"Back To The Days Of The Romans"	
44240	"Gina"/"Escape"	

Buddah

116	"I'm Gonna Make You Mine"/"I'm Gonna Get Married"	1969
149	"Are You Getting Any Sunshine"/"It'll Take Time"	

Twist on Down

⦿

"The Twist," and the other offshoot dances spawned by it, played a part in keeping rock and roll alive during the early 60's. In the absolute forefront of "The Twist" was Chubby Checker.

CHUBBY CHECKER

The undisputed early 60's twist sultan, Chubby Checker recorded the phenomenally popular version of the Hank Ballard stage dance for his group, The Midnighters.

Chubby Checker's first two Parkway label releases were poor selling, novelty efforts. The most successful was "The Class," the label of which read "Chubby Checker imitating Fats Domino, The Coasters, Elvis Presley and The Chipmonks (sic)" in a rowdy "Charlie Brown" classroom setting. It was "The Twist," however, a national hit in 1960 and a national craze in 1962, that rocketed Chubby Checker into the flashy forefront of the early 60's discotheque scene.

Checker's next fifteen or so single recordings were assorted dances, either variations on "The Twist" such as "Twistin' U.S.A.," "Let's Twist Again" and "Slow Twistin'"; along with other dance steps, including the most popular "Pony Time," a Don Covay original, "The Fly" and "The Popeye." By the mid-60's, the discotheque fervor had cooled, with it went the popularity of Chubby Checker and other artists who depended upon the beat of "The Twist."

Values

By far the scarcest and most valuable singles by Chubby Checker are those 45's which were issued before the name of Chubby Checker was synonymous with "The Twist." "Samson And Delilah" and the more sought-after "The Class," on the original white Parkway label can attract $8 to $10. "The Twist" on this same white Parkway label is also rare and can bring over $5; on the orange label, with the original "Toot" flip, the record fetches $2 to $3. Later Chubby Checker issues bring $2 or less—picture sleeves give these singles a firmer $2 value.

Discography

Parkway

804	"The Class"/"Schooldays, Oh Schooldays"	1959
808	"Samson & Delilah"/"Whole Lotta Laughin'"	
810	"Those Private Eyes (Keep Watching Me)"/"Dancing Dinosaur"	
811	"The Twist"/"Toot" (reissued in 1961 on Parkway 811 as "The Twist"/"Let's Twist Again")	1960
813	"The Hucklebuck"/"Whole Lotta Shakin' Goin' On"	

818 "Pony Time"/"Oh Susannah" 1961
822 "Good Good Lovin'"/"The Mess Around"
824 "Let's Twist Again"/"Everything's Gonna Be All Right"
830 "The Fly"/"That's The Way It Goes"
835 "Slow Twistin'"/"La Paloma Twist" 1962
842 "Dancin' Party"/"Gotta Get Myself Together"
849 "Limbo Rock"/"Popeye"
862 "Let's Limbo Some More"/"Twenty Miles" 1963
873 "Bird Land"/"Black Cloud"
879 "Surf Party"/"Twist It Up"
890 "Loddy Lo"/"Hooka Tooka"
907 "Hey Bobba Needle"/"Spread Joy" 1964
920 "Lazy Elsie Molly"/"Rosie"
922 "She Wants T'Swim"/"You Better Believe It"
936 "Loverly Loverly"/"The Weekend's Here"
949 "Do The Freddie"/"At The Discotheque" 1965
959 "Everything's Wrong"/"Cu Ma La Be—Stay"
989 "Hey You Little Boo-Ga-Loo"/"Pussy Cat" 1966
105 "You Got The Power"/"Looking At Tomorrow"
112 "Karate Monkey"/"Her Heart"

Buddah
100 "Back In The USSR"/"Windy Cream" 1969

JOEY DEE AND THE STARLITERS

Joey Dee And The Starliters were second only to Chubby Checker when it came to cashing in on the twist mania. Early, pre-twist recordings by Joey Dee are in the tradition of the New York area "do-wop" vocal groups, with a style similar to that of Dion And The Belmonts or The Mystics. Joey Dee's tightly harmonic ballads met with only cool regional success. "The Peppermint Twist," though, was a major twist hit, giving the New York discotheque scene a national boost. Joey Dee And The Starliters, like Chubby Checker, had several twist beat hits, then sharply declined in popularity in the mid-60's.

Values

At best, early Joey Dee records were limited regional successes, thus his recordings on Bonus, Scepter and Jubilee are valued from $3 to $5. The Roulette label twist era hits, with picture sleeve, generally bring about $2.

Discography

As by Joey Dee:

Dot

15699	"Somebody Sweet"	1958

Bonus

7009	"Lorraine"	

Scepter

1210	"Face Of An Angel"/"Shimmy Baby"	1960

As by Joey Dee And The Starliters:

Jubilee

5539	"Dancing On The Beach"/"Good Little You"	1963
5554	"She's So Exceptional"/"It's Got You"	
5566	"You Can't Sit Down"/"Put Your Heart In It"	

Roulette

4401	"Peppermint Twist Pt. 1 & Pt. 2"	1961

4408 "Hey, Let's Twist"/"Roly Poly" 1962
4416 "Shout Pt. 1 & 2"
4431 "Everytime Pt. 1 & 2"
4438 "What Kind Of Love Is This"/"Wing Ding"
4456 "I Lost My Baby"/"Keep Your Mind On What You're Doin'"
4467 "Baby You're Driving Me Crazy"/"Help Me Pick Up The Pieces" 1963
4488 "Hot Pastrami With Mashed Potatoes Pt. 1 & Pt. 2"
4503 "Dance, Dance, Dance"/"Let's Have A Party"
4525 "Ya Ya"/"Fannie Mae"

As by Joey Dee:

Roulette
4539 "Getting Nearer"/"Down By The Riverside"

Bubble Gum Rock and Roll

Bubble Gum Rock And Roll is best described as the sound achieved from a media-crafted recording package designed for a teenage and pre-teen listening market. The Monkees of 1966 were the first and best-known example of such a Bubble Gum creation. The sound made by The Monkees was crisp and good and was occasionally solid rock and roll. Other groups with this likable pre-teen sound, though not similarly media-packaged, included The Buckinghams, The Box Tops and Tommy James And The Shondells. By 1967, Bubble Gum Rock evolved into an even more elementary sound with the popularity of recordings designed for the nursery school/cartoon set. The Ohio Express, The 1910 Fruitgum Company, The Lemon Pipers and The Archies all succeeded and thrived for the balance of the 60's performing this Nursery Rhyme Rock.

THE MONKEES

A totally pre-programmed, media-packaged rock and roll unit, The Monkees arrived on the rock and roll scene with some surprisingly tasteful and entirely optimistic singles. None of the death or depression rock and roll for The Monkees, their approach was strictly bright and upbeat. In particular, the initial releases "Last Train To Clarksville" and "I'm A Believer" were not only hits but were professional rock and roll. The Monkees were thrust into mercurial superstardom. After all, they were handpicked to capitalize rapidly in several areas: record sales, a TV program, concerts and all the merchandising associated with a rock group that is heavily promoted. Each Monkees single was a hit, but the hit string was short. The last hits were the ballad "Valleri" and the novelty "D.W. Washburn." By 1968, the cotton candy Monkees were over the hill. Perhaps their two years of popularity had exceeded the fondest wishes of their promoters. But, finally, The Monkees had given way to the new generation of Nursery Rhyme rockers.

Values

Singles by The Monkees are just now attracting demand, they are worth $2 apiece, with a picture sleeve.

Discography

Colgems

1001	"Last Train To Clarksville"/"Take A Giant Step"	1966
1002	"I'm A Believer"/"Stepping Stone"	

1004 "A Little Bit Me, A Little Bit You"/"The Girl I Knew Somewhere" 1967
1007 "Pleasant Valley Sunday"/"Words"
1012 "Daydream Believer"/"Goin' Down"
1019 "Valleri"/"Tapioca Tundra" 1968
1023 "D.W. Washburn"/"It's Nice To Be With You"
1031 "Porpoise Song"/"As We Go Along"
5000 "Teardrop City"/"A Man Without A Dream"
5004 "Listen To The Band"/"Someday Man" 1969
5005 "Good Clean Fun"/"Mommy And Daddy"
5011 "Oh My My"/"I Love You Better"

THE BUCKINGHAMS

The Buckinghams were the best-known exponents of a short-lived Chicago pop rock and roll sound. The Buckinghams, at first recording for the small Chicago U.S.A. label, had a fast tempo hit in "Kind Of A Drag." Moving to the Columbia label, The Buckinghams scored with four upbeat successes: "Don't You Care," "Hey Baby (They're Playing Our Song)," "Susan" and "Mercy, Mercy, Mercy," a vocal remake of the Cannonball Adderly down-home instrumental.

Values

Singles by The Buckinghams on the U.S.A. label generally bring about $2, while their several hits on Columbia are below this $2 level.

Discography

U.S.A.
844 "Don't Want To Cry"/"I'll Go Crazy" 1965

848 "I Call Your Name"/"Makin' Up And Breakin' Up"
860 "Kind Of A Drag"/"You Make Me Feel So Good" 1966
869 "Lawdy Miss Clawdy"/"Making Up And Breaking Up" 1967

Columbia
44053 "Don't You Care"/"Why Don't You Love Me" 1967
44182 "Mercy, Mercy, Mercy"/"You Are Gone"
44254 "Hey Baby"/"And Our Love"
44378 "Susan"/"Foreign Policy"
44533 "Back In Love Again"/"You Misunderstand Me" 1968
44672 "Where Did You Come From"/"Song Of The Breeze"
44923 "Difference Of Opinion"/"It's A Beautiful Day"

Laurie
3258 "Gonna Say Goodbye"/"Many Times"

TOMMY JAMES AND THE SHONDELLS

Tommy James And The Shondells had immediate success with the rock and roll stomper, "Hanky Panky," a reissue on the Roulette label. Hits by Tommy James And The Shondells were mainly of the good time, upbeat variety, with "I Think We're Alone Now" and "Gettin' Together," both 1967 releases, and "Mony Mony" in 1968. By 1968, Tommy James And The Shondells had become a major American pop rock and roll group. They adjusted their style —attempting polished poetry—and did well with such sparkling ballads as "Crimson And Clover" and "Crystal Blue Persuasion." Tommy James And The Shondells were credited with some fine late 60's and early 70's rockers, especially the 1970 release of the engaging "Draggin' The Line" (Roulette 7103).

Values

The original pressing of "Hanky Panky" by The Shondells on the small Snap label can bring up to $5, while the Roulette label reissue brings $2 or less. Later Roulette issues are in the same price range.

Discography

As by The Shondells:

Snap

102	"Hanky Panky"/"Thunderbolt"	1966

As by Tommy James And The Shondells:

Roulette

4686	"Hanky Panky"/"Thunderbolt"	1966
4695	"Say I Am"/"Lots Of Pretty Girls"	
4710	"It's Only Love"/"Don't Let My Love Pass You By"	
4720	"I Think We're Alone Now"/"Gone Gone Gone"	1967
4736	"Mirage"/"Run Run Baby Run"	
4756	"I Like The Way"/"Baby I Can't Take It No More"	
4762	"Gettin' Together"/"Real Girl"	
4775	"Out Of The Blue"/"Love's Closin' In On Me"	
7000	"Get Out Now"/"Wish It Were You"	1968
7008	"Mony Mony"/"One, Two, Three And I Fell"	
7016	"Somebody Cares"/"Do Unto Me"	

7024 "Do Something To Me"/"Gingerbread Man"
7028 "Crimson And Clover"/"Some Kind Of Love"
7039 "Sweet Cherry Wine"/"Breakaway" 1969
7050 "Crystal Blue Persuasion"/"I'm Alive"
7060 "Balls Of Fire"/"Makin' Good Time"
7066 "She"/"Loved One"
7071 "Red Rover"/"Gotta Get Back To You"
7076 "Come To Me"/"Talkin' And Signifyin'"

THE BOX TOPS

The Box Tops achieved a pinnacle of popularity in 1967 with two fine rock and roll hits, "The Letter" and "Cry Like A Baby." Other single releases also sold fairly well, including the slow rock beat "Choo Choo Train" and the Bob Dylan classic, "I Shall Be Released."

Values

Records by The Box Tops are valued below $2.

Discography

Mala
565 "The Letter"/"Happy Times" 1967
580 "Neon Rainbow"/"Everything I Am"
593 "Cry Like A Baby"/"The Door You Closed To Me" 1968
12005 "Choo Choo Train"/"Fields Of Clover"
12017 "I Met Her In Church"/"People Gonna Talk"

12035	"Sweet Cream Ladies March Forward"/ "I See Only Sunshine"	
12038	"I Shall Be Released"/"Must Be The Devil"	1969
12040	"Soul Deep"/"Happy Song"	
12042	"Turn On A Dream"/"Together"	

Nursery Rhyme Rock

⦿

Nursery Rhyme Rock is a fitting description for the recorded works of four vocal groups, The Ohio Express, The 1910 Fruitgum Co., The Lemon Pipers and The Archies.

These groups were popular at a point in rock history when heavy "acid" rock was dominant. Nursery Rhyme Rock was a perfect antidote to this power rock and met a need for innocent lyrics with performances devoid of bluster and pretension.

THE OHIO EXPRESS

The Ohio Express, the earliest of the Nursery Rhyme Rock groups, originally recorded for Cameo of Philadelphia. The Express developed hit appeal with good backbeat rock and roll, this gave them several hits on the emerging Buddah label. The incessant beat of "Yummy Yummy Yummy" and "Chewy Chewy" were little more than sing-song lyrics with catchy rhymes; there was no attempt at weightier expression.

Values

The Cameo label issues by The Ohio Express can bring around $2, while the more contemporary and more successful Buddah label releases are worth under $2.

Discography

Cameo		
483	"Beg, Borrow And Steal"/"Maybe"	1967
2001	"Try It"/"Soul Struttin'"	1968
Buddah		
38	"Yummy, Yummy, Yummy"/"Zig Zag"	1968
56	"Down At Lulu's"/"She's Not Comin' Home"	
70	"Chewy Chewy"/"Firebird"	
92	"Sweeter Than Sugar"/"Bitter Lemon"	1969
102	"Mercy"/"Roll It Up"	
117	"Pinch Me"/"Peanuts"	
129	"Sausalito"/"Make Love, Not War"	

THE 1910 FRUITGUM COMPANY

The 1910 Fruitgum Company specialized in adapting rhyming games played by preadolescents. They turned these simple phrases into rock and roll lyrics: "Simon Says," "May I Take A Giant Step" and "1,2,3 Red Light"—all were hits as innocent as the games portrayed. The sound of The Fruitgum Company tended more toward middle-of-the-road pop than the rocking sound of The Ohio Express.

Values

The Super K label release by The 1910 Fruitgum Company can bring up to $2 from collectors of this sound. Later Buddah label issues remain under $2.

Discography

Super K

15	"Go Away"/"The Track"	1967

Buddah

24	"Simon Says"/"Reflections From The Looking Glass"	1968
39	"May I Take A Giant Step"/"Mr. Jensen"	
54	"1,2,3 Red Light"/"Sticky Sticky"	
71	"Goody Goody Gumdrops"/"Candy Kisses"	
91	"Indian Giver"/"Pow Wow"	1969
114	"Special Delivery"/"No Good Annie"	
130	"The Train"/"Eternal Light"	
146	"When We Get Married"/"Baby Bret"	

THE LEMON PIPERS

The Lemon Pipers were the third of the major Buddah label Nursery Rhyme vocal groups. This lightweight unit scored with one major hit, "Green Tambourine" and two minor upbeat successes, "Rice Is Nice" and "Jelly Jungle," completely innocent material.

Values

The several singles by The Lemon Pipers remain well below $2.

Discography

Buddah

23	"Green Tambourine"/"No Help From Me"	1968
31	"Rice Is Nice"/"Blueberry Blue"	
41	"Jelly Jungle"/"Shoeshine Boy"	
63	"Wine & Violet"/"Lonely Atmosphere"	

THE ARCHIES

The Archies were the only vocal group created expressly for a popular TV cartoon series. The recorded material by The Archies was upbeat and happy in content. They scored one major hit, "Sugar Sugar," in 1968.

Values

Singles by The Archies have not exceeded a $2 ceiling.

Discography

Calendar

1006	"Bang-Shang-A Lang"/"Truck Driver"	1968
1007	"Feelin' So Good"/"Love Light"	
1008	"Sugar Sugar"/"Melody Hill"	

Kirshner

1009	"Sunshine"/"Over And Over"	1968
5002	"Jingle Jangle"/"Justine"	1969
5003	"Who's Your Baby"/"Senorita Rita"	
5009	"Together We Two"/"Everything's Alright"	
5011	"Throw A Little Love My Way"/"This Is Love"	

Reissues

Many of the very biggest pop rock and roll hits of the 50's and 60's remain available on 45 RPM. However, they are not on the original labels but on special reissue labels. The following discography lists those hits by artists reviewed in this work which have been preserved and are currently available.

THE COVER RECORD

Pat Boone

Dot

107 "Moody River"/"Speedy Gonzales"
108 "Ain't That A Shame"/"Friendly Persuasion"
109 "April Love"/"Don't Forbid Me"
110 "A Wonderful Time Up There"/"Love Letters In The Sand"
151 "I Almost Lost My Mind"/"I'll Be Home"
242 "The Exodus Song"

The Crew Cuts

Mercury Celebrity Series
30048 "Sh Boom"/"Earth Angel"

The Cheers

Capitol Star Line Series
6212 "Black Denim Trousers And Motorcycle Boots"/ "Bazoom"

The Diamonds

Mercury Celebrity Series
30050 "Little Darlin'"/"The Church Bells May Ring"

NOVELTY RECORDS

David Seville

UA Silver Spotlight Series
063 "The Witch Doctor"/"The Bird On My Head"

The Chipmunks

UA Silver Spotlight Series
056 "The Chipmunk Song"/"Ragtime Cowboy Joe"
057 "Alvin's Harmonica"/"Rudolph The Red Nosed Reindeer"

Nervous Norvous

Dot
130 "Transfusion"/"Dig"

The Hollywood Argyles

Era Back To Back Hits
011 "Alley Oop"/"Hully Gully"

Larry Verne

Era Back To Back Hits
004 "Mr. Custer"/"Mr. Livingston"

Bobby "Boris" Pickett

Parrot
348 "Monster Mash"/"Monster's Mash Party"
366 "Monster's Holiday"

ROCKABILLY ROOTS

The Everly Brothers

Barnaby
605 "Like Strangers"/"Brand New Heartache"
606 "Be Bop A Lula"/"When Will I Be Loved"
607 "Let It Be Me"/"Take A Message To Mary"
608 "(Til) I Kissed You"/"Oh What A Feeling"
609 "All I Have To Do Is Dream"/"Claudette"
610 "Bird Dog"/"Devoted To You"
611 "Bye Bye Love"/"Problems"
612 "Wake Up Little Susie"/"Maybe Tomorrow"
613 "This Little Girl Of Mine"/"Should We Tell Him"

Warner Brothers Back To Back Hits
7110 "Cathy's Clown"/"So Sad"
7111 "Lucille"/"Crying In The Rain"
0314 "Ebony Eyes"/"Walk Right Back"

George Hamilton IV

ABC Goldies 45
1469 "A Rose And A Baby Ruth"/"Why Don't They Understand"

Bobby Helms

Kapp Winner Circle Series
85 "Jingle Bell Rock"/"The Bell That Couldn't Jingle"

MCA
60026 "Fraulein"/"My Special Angel"

Brenda Lee

MCA
60069 "Sweet Nothin's"/"I Want To Be Wanted"
60070 "I'm Sorry"/"All Alone Am I"
60088 "As Usual"/"Too Many Rivers"

Jimmy Bowen

Roulette Golden Goodies
14 "I'm Stickin' With You"/"Warm Up To Me Baby"

Buddy Knox

Roulette Golden Goodies
42 "Party Doll"

ABC Goldies 45
2516 "My Baby's Gone"

UA Silver Spotlight Series
040 "Lovey Dovey"/"Ling Ting Tong"

EARLY TEEN IDOLS

Bobby Darin

Atlantic Oldies Series
13055 "Splish Splash"/"Queen Of The Hop"
13056 "Beyond The Sea"/"Moritat"
13057 "Dream Lover"/"If I Were A Carpenter"

Ricky Nelson

UA Silver Spotlight Series
071 "Be Bop Baby"/"Stood Up"
072 "Lonesome Town"/"It's Up To You"
073 "Poor Little Fool"/"My Bucket's Got A Hole In It"
074 "Travelin' Man"/"Believe What You Say"
075 "Teenage Idol"/"Young Emotions"
076 "Never Be Anyone Else But You"/"That's All"
077 "Young World"/"It's Late"
078 "Waitin' In School"/"Just A Little Too Much"
079 "Hello Mary Lou"/"Sweeter Than You"
080 "A Wonder Like You"/"Everlovin'"

MOVIE STAR ROCK AND ROLL

Tab Hunter

Dot
121 "Young Love"/"Ninety Nine Ways"

ROCK AND ROLL VOCAL GROUPS

The Four Seasons

Phillips Golden Hit Series
44010 "Rag Doll"/"Ronnie"
44011 "Dawn"/"Save It For Me"
44017 "Sherry"/"Big Man In Town"
44018 "Big Girls Don't Cry"/"Opus 17"
44019 "Walk Like A Man"/"Girl Come Running"
44020 "Let's Hang On"/"Working My Way Back To You"
44021 "I've Got You Under My Skin"/"Bye Bye Baby"
44022 "Candy Girl"/"Peanuts"
44024 "Marlena"/"Stay"

The Crests

ABC Goldies 45
2583 "Trouble In Paradise"/"Always You"
2584 "Step By Step"/"Gee"
2585 "The Angels Listened In"/"I Thank The Moon"
2586 "Six Nights A Week"/"I Do"
2587 "16 Candles"/"Beside You"

The Brooklyn Bridge

Radio Active Gold
10 "Worst That Could Happen"

Danny And The Juniors

ABC Goldies 45
2411 "At The Hop"/"Rock And Roll Is Here To Stay"

Dion And The Timberlanes

Virgo
6032 "The Chosen Few"

Dion

Columbia Hall Of Fame
33060 "Ruby Baby"/"Donna The Prima Donna"
33220 "Drip Drop"/"This Little Girl"

The Tokens

RCA Gold Standard
0702 "The Lion Sleeps Tonight"/"B'wa Nina"
Radio Active Gold
20 "She Lets Her Hair Down"
51 "Tonight I Fell In Love"/"I'll Always Love You"
53 "The Lion Sleeps Tonight"/"Beautiful People"
ABC Goldies 45
2550 "Tonight I Fell In Love"/"I'll Always Love You"

Neil Sedaka

RCA Gold Standard
0575 "Oh Carol"/"Calendar Girl"
0597 "The Diary"/"Happy Birthday Sweet 16"
0701 "Breaking Up Is Hard To Do"/"Next Door To An Angel"
0939 "Little Devil"/"Stairway To Heaven"

The Playmates

Roulette Golden Goodies
47 "Beep Beep"/"What Is Love"
75 "Jo-Ann"/"Wait For Me"

The Royal Teens

Roulette Golden Goodies
126 "Short Shorts"

ABC Goldies 45
2402 "Short Shorts"

The Teddy Bears

Era Back To Back Hits
008 "To Know Him Is To Love Him"

The Fleetwoods

UA Silver Spotlight Series
038 "Come Softly To Me"/"Runaround"
039 "Mr. Blue"
515 "Goodnight My Love"
526 "(He's) The Great Imposter"

The Echoes

Roulette Golden Goodies
4 "Baby Blue"

Jay And The Americans

UA Silver Spotlight Series
026 "She Cried"/"Come A Little Bit Closer"
027 "Cara Mia"/"Let's Lock The Door"
028 "This Magic Moment"/"Walking In The Rain"

The Regents

Roulette Golden Goodies
5 "Barbara Ann"

ABC Goldies 45
2520 "Barbara Ann"/"I'm So Lonely"

PHILADELPHIA ROCK AND ROLL

Frankie Avalon

ABC Goldies 45
2623 "Venus"/"I'm Broke"
2632 "Bobby Sox To Stockings"/"A Boy Without A Girl"

Fabian

ABC Goldies 45
2624 "Turn Me Loose"/"Stop Thief"
2625 "Tiger"/"Mighty Cold"

Billie And Lillie

ABC Goldies 45
2578 "La Dee Dah"/"The Monster"
2579 "Lucky Lady Bug"/"I Promise You"

Bobby Rydell

Abko
4007 "The Cha Cha Cha"/"Wildwood Days"
4008 "Wild One"/"Swingin' School"
4009 "Kissin' Time"/"We Got Love"

WEST COAST ROCK AND ROLL

Jan And Dean

UA Silver Spotlight Series
- 089 "Baby Talk"/"Jennie Lee"
- 090 "Linda"/"New Girl In School"
- 091 "Surf City"/"Ride The Wild Surf"
- 092 "Drag City"/"Dead Man's Curve"
- 093 "Honolulu Lulu"/"Sidewalk Surfin'"
- 094 "The Little Old Lady From Pasadena"/"Popsicle"

The Beach Boys

Capitol Star Line Series
- 6059 "Be True To Your School"/"In My Room"
- 6081 "Help Me Rhonda"/"Do You Wanna Dance"
- 6095 "Surfin' Safari"/"409"
- 6105 "Dance Dance Dance"/"The Warmth Of The Sun"
- 6106 "Fun Fun Fun"/"Do It Again"
- 6107 "Surfer Girl"/"Little Deuce Coupe"

PACIFIC NORTHWEST ROCK AND ROLL

Paul Revere And The Raiders

Columbia Hall Of Fame
- 33082 "Louie Louie"/"Louie Go Home"
- 33098 "Kicks"/"Just Like Me"
- 33106 "Hungry"/"The Great Airplane Strike"
- 33111 "Good Thing"/"Ups And Downs"
- 33126 "Steppin' Out"/"Him Or Me—What's It Gonna Be"
- 33137 "Don't Take It So Hard"/"Cinderella Sunshine"
- 33162 "Cinderella Sunshine"/"Mr. Sun Mr. Moon"

33171 "Let Me"/"We Gotta Get It All Together"

The Kingsmen

Scepter Wand Forever
21011 "Louie Louie"/"Haunted Castle"
21012 "Money"/"Little Latin Lupe Lu"

ROCKABILLY ROOTS II

Jimmy Clanton

ABC Goldies 45
2470 "Just A Dream"/"You Aim To Please"
2473 "Go Jimmy Go"/"I Trusted You"
2474 "Venus In Blue Jeans"/"Highway Bound"

Bobby Vee

UA Silver Spotlight Series
020 "Devil Or Angel"/"Stayin' In"
021 "Rubber Ball"/"Punish Her"
022 "Take Good Care Of My Baby"/"Please Don't Ask About Barbara"
023 "Run To Him"/"Sharing You"
024 "The Night Has A Thousand Eyes"/"Charms"
025 "Come Back When You Grow Up"/"Beautiful People"

Tommy Roe

ABC Goldies 45
1446 "Sheila"/"Sweet Pea"
1447 "Dizzy"/"Hooray For Hazel"
1448 "Heather Honey"/"Jam Up Jelly Tight"

The Fireballs

Dot
238 "Sugar Shack"/"Daisy Petal Pickin'"

Atlantic Oldies Series
13078 "Bottle Of Wine"/"Long Green"

Ral Donner

Roulette Golden Goodies
19 "You Don't Know What You've Got Until You Lose It"/"She's Everything"
97 "Girl Of My Best Friend"/"To Love Somebody"

ABC Goldies 45
2489 "Girl Of My Best Friend"/"It's Been A Long Long Time"
2490 "You Don't Know What You've Got Until You Lose It"/"So Close To Heaven"

Johnny Rivers

UA Silver Spotlight Series
101 "Memphis"/"Secret Agent Man"
102 "Mountain Of Love"/"Maybellene"
103 "Seventh Son"/"Midnight Special"
104 "Poor Side Of Town"/"Baby I Need Your Lovin'"
105 "Summer Rain"/"The Tracks Of My Tears"

The Bobby Fuller 4

Era Back To Back Hits
032 "I Fought The Law"

Lou Christie

Roulette Golden Goodies
6 "The Gypsy Cried"/"Two Faces Have I"

ABC Goldies 45
2497 "Two Faces Have I"/"All That Glitters Isn't Gold"
2498 "The Gypsy Cried"/"Red Sails In The Sunset"

MGM Golden Circle
185 "Lightning Strikes"/"Rhapsody In The Rain"

TWIST ON DOWN

Chubby Checker

Abko
4001 "The Twist"/"Loddy Lo"
4002 "The Hucklebuck"/"Pony Time"
4004 "Hey Bobba Needle"/"Hooka Tooka"

Joey Dee And The Starliters

Roulette Golden Goodies
28 "Peppermint Twist Pt. 1 & Pt. 2"
29 "Shout Pt. 1 & Pt. 2"
36 "Hot Pastrami With Mashed Potatoes Pt. 1 & Pt. 2"

ABC Goldies 45
2491 "What Kind Of Love Is This"/"Wing Ding"
2492 "Shout Pt. 1 & Pt. 2"
2493 "Peppermint Twist Pt. 1 & Pt. 2"

BUBBLE GUM ROCK AND ROLL

The Monkees

Flashback
70 "Last Train To Clarksville"/"Monkee's Theme"
71 "I'm A Believer"/"Pleasant Valley Sunday"
72 "Stepping Stone"/"Daydream Believer"

The Buckinghams

Columbia Hall Of Fame
33118 "Don't You Care"/"Mercy Mercy Mercy"
33132 "Hey Baby"/"Susan"
33155 "Kind Of A Drag"/"Back In Love Again"

Tommy James And The Shondells

Roulette Golden Goodies
17 "Hanky Panky"/"Gettin' Together"
71 "I Think We're Alone Now"/"Say I Am"
72 "Crimson And Clover"
73 "Mony Mony"/"Crystal Blue Persuasion"
78 "I Like The Way"/"Mirage"
103 "Do Something To Me"/"I'm Alive"

ABC Goldies 45
2482 "Crystal Blue Persuasion"/"I'm Alive"
2483 "Crimson And Clover"/"Taken"
2505 "Mony Mony"/"One Two Three And I Fell"
2506 "I Think We're Alone Now"/"Gone Gone Gone"
2507 "Hanky Panky"/"Thunderbolt"

The Box Tops

Flashback
38 "Cry Like A Baby"/"The Door You Closed To Me"
39 "The Letter"/"Happy Times"
44 "Neon Rainbow"/"Everything I Am"
53 "Choo Choo Train"/"Soul Deep"

NURSERY RHYME ROCK

The Ohio Express

Radio Active Gold
4 "Yummy Yummy Yummy"/"Zig Zag"

6 "Down At Lulu's"/"She's Not Comin' Home"
8 "Chewy Chewy"/"Firebird"
12 "Sweeter Than Sugar"/"Cowboy Convention"
14 "Mercy"/"Roll It Up"

The 1910 Fruitgum Company

Radio Active Gold
2 "Simon Says"/"Reflections From The Looking Glass"
5 "1,2,3 Red Light"/"Sticky Sticky"
9 "Goody Goody Gumdrops"/"Candy Kisses"
11 "Indian Giver"/"May I Take A Giant Step"
15 "Special Delivery"/"No Good Annie"
17 "The Train"/"Eternal Light"

The Lemon Pipers

Radio Active Gold
1 "Green Tambourine"/"No Help From Me"
3 "Rice Is Nice"/"Blueberry Blue"
20 "Green Tambourine"

The Archies

RCA Gold Standard
0930 "Sugar Sugar"/"Feelin' So Good"
0931 "Jingle Jangle"/"Bang-Shang-A-Lang"